Praise for *A Monk's Guide to Happiness*

'Thubten is a very generous and kind monk who writes with the lived honesty and humour of someone who has experienced the wisdom he shares. His writing is full of inspiration but also the pragmatism needed to form a sustainable practice. His book clearly illustrates why we all need meditation and mindfulness in our lives.'
Benedict Cumberbatch

'Matt and I have both completely fallen in love with Thubten's outlook on life and his way of creating a genuine sense of happiness. His meditations have been a game-changer too. I really couldn't recommend this book more highly.'   **Ella Mills, founder of Deliciously Ella**

'Gelong Thubten's wonderful book provides a bracing challenge to our search for instant gratification and "instant" happiness, and a lucid, practical, step-by-step path to contentment and a genuine and lasting peace of mind.'
Mick Brown, journalist for *The Daily Telegraph*

'Compelling to read, yet full of profound wisdom, this wonderful book rationally describes how our mind functions and how we can cultivate the habit of happiness.'
Professor Lokesh Joshi, Vice President for Research, National University of Ireland

Dedicated to
Akong Tulku Rinpoche
and my mother

A Monk's Guide To Happiness

Meditation in the 21st century

Gelong Thubten

First published in Great Britain in 2019 by Yellow Kite
An imprint of Hodder & Stoughton
An Hachette UK company

This paperback edition published in 2020

5

A CIP catalogue record for this title is available from the British Library

Paperback ISBN 978 1 473 69668 6
eBook ISBN 978 1 473 69669 3

Typeset in Celeste by
Palimpsest Book Production Ltd, Falkirk, Stirlingshire

Printed and bound in Great Britain by Clays Ltd, Elcograf S.p.A.

Hodder & Stoughton policy is to use papers that are natural,
renewable and recyclable products and made from wood grown
in sustainable forests. The logging and manufacturing processes
are expected to conform to the environmental regulations
of the country of origin.

Yellow Kite
Hodder & Stoughton Ltd
Carmelite House
50 Victoria Embankment
London EC4Y 0DZ

www.yellowkitebooks.co.uk

Contents

CHAPTER ONE: What is Happiness?   1

CHAPTER TWO: Hard-wired to be Happy   13

CHAPTER THREE: Stress in the 21st Century   23

CHAPTER FOUR: Meditation and Mindfulness   41

CHAPTER FIVE: Getting Started   63

CHAPTER SIX: Building the Habit   87

CHAPTER SEVEN: Going Deeper   111

CHAPTER EIGHT: Happiness is a Group Effort   135

CHAPTER NINE: Compassion   161

CHAPTER TEN: Forgiveness   191

CHAPTER ELEVEN: Energising Your Practice   213

Afterword   243

Acknowledgements   245

CHAPTER ONE

What is Happiness?

• • •

In June 2009 I emerged from a meditation retreat that had lasted four years. It was an intensive programme alongside 20 other monks, in a remote old farmhouse on the Isle of Arran in Scotland. We were completely cut off from the outside world, with no phones, Internet or newspapers. Food was brought in by a caretaker who lived outside the walls of the retreat and we had a strict schedule of between 12 and 14 hours' meditation per day, mostly practised alone in our rooms. This programme went on in the same way every day for four years. We were allowed to talk a little to each other at mealtimes or in the short breaks between sessions, but things intensified in the second year, when we took a vow of silence for five months.

I had never attempted such a long retreat before, and it was incredibly hard. I remember thinking it was like having open-heart surgery with no anaesthetic: you're backed into the corner with your most painful thoughts and feelings, with no distraction or escape. This type of retreat is a radical method of meditation training, found in many Tibetan Buddhist monasteries. The completely immersive environment and intense schedule of long meditation sessions push the meditator to make friends with their own mind. At times, it was the unhappiest period of my life, yet in the end it taught me a lot about happiness. I learned that happiness is a *choice*, and something that we can tap into within ourselves.

The other monks and I had no idea what was happening in the outside world. Several things occurred during this period which have impacted upon our culture, including game-changing technologies such as the launch and widespread use of the iPhone, the arrival of YouTube, Twitter and Facebook, as well as major historical events such as the election of President Obama, the financial crisis and the execution of Saddam Hussein. Our retreat teacher would come in to check on us every few months, and did hint at some pieces of news: we were told there was this 'thing called Facebook where people ask you to be friends with them, and you feel too guilty to say no'; hearing this, we simply stared in wide-eyed wonder.

When I came out, back into the 'normal' world, one of the main things I noticed was the speed of things; everything and everyone moved so fast. Smartphones had become ubiquitous; the BlackBerry was now a dinosaur. Walking through London, I felt as if I had landed in a 'zombie apocalypse'. It seemed people were wandering about in a hypnotic trance, their faces buried in screens. I also noticed that in the London underground train stations, the advertising posters lining the walls beside the escalators were now moving digital images, and I felt dizzy as they flew past me. People 'out here' had maybe not felt the temperature rising, but my retreat and re-emergence gave me a fresh perspective on how things had sped up. I also sensed a change in mood: most of the news now had a slightly hysterical tone, dominated by horror stories constantly invading people's phones, leaving them with no escape. In the 21st century our relationship with information has completely changed; we know far too much. Even the way we consume information – in fleeting, bite-sized chunks through 'scrolling' and 'swiping' – has altered the landscape of how we process reality.

Emerging from the retreat, I was also struck by how people's use of instant gratification as a means of feeling 'happy' had reached new heights and how dissatisfied they were still feeling. As I started to interact with things, I got a strong sense that meditation was exactly what the world needed now, and not as a luxury but as a matter of survival. I became passionate about the pressing question of true, lasting happiness and what that really meant. So with a deeper sense of commitment, I immersed myself in teaching meditation in diverse environments, such as schools, universities, hospitals, drug-rehabilitation centres and prisons, as well as in global technology companies and numerous highly stressed workplaces.

THE HAPPINESS 'HIT'

I've found that many people seek a kind of happiness which is a fleeting sensation: a 'high' – an injection-like bolt of energy to the heart. Yet this never seems to last, and when they no longer experience that high, they crave it again.

We live in times where there's a lot of emphasis on feeling good. We look for some kind of 'hit', like a sugar rush, and so we lurch from one 'buzz' to the next, concerned with having our senses stimulated and satisfied, sometimes all of them at once.

Much of the food and drink we consume creates an instant, false boost: sugar, additives, coffee, 'comfort carbs' . . . We feel tired in the middle of the afternoon and so we grab a bar of chocolate and/or some caffeine to make ourselves feel better. There's an advert for a particular brand of crisps with the tagline, 'Once you pop, you can't stop' – and sure enough, the ingredients in the product can make us eat our way through an entire pack in one go. Do we ever find long-term satisfaction?

Watching films and television programmes made today compared with those from the past, one of the main differences you see is that the modern style of filming tends to use exciting, fast-moving imagery which stimulates the senses. Films, television programmes, commercials and music videos can have hundreds of different frames squeezed into two minutes, and much of this is because we're highly distracted and addicted to having our senses ramped up. An old black-and-white movie, where the camera lingers for a long time on one shot, seems boring; we now call that 'art house', it's not the mainstream. We are drawn nowadays to a jumpy and excitable experience, which reflects how we live.

Social media has enabled a huge sense of connection but at the same time deep isolation. Lost in our screens, we scroll through images of other people eating their lunch while we eat ours, and we find it more and more boring just to sit still and be in the moment. It's hard for us to have simple experiences anymore; instead we crave the multiple inputs of eating while watching television or looking at social media and listening to music. We quickly find things dull, and so we constantly grab at the next experience, yet we never seem to fully arrive at it. We've become addicted to 'likes', to the latest shiny material object or to *anything* that we think might bring us a pleasant feeling. We feel tired, our systems running on the stress hormones cortisol and adrenaline. Our bodies become overloaded with toxic chemistry, which we keep feeding, making us exhausted, unwell and wanting more. Craving leads to more craving as we perpetuate an endless habit, whereby nothing is actually satisfying because the mind has already jumped over it in pursuit of the next thing. It's like an endless hunger, where we are constantly asking, 'When is it all going to happen for me? When am I going to feel fulfilled? What's the next thing?' Is *this* happiness?

The main brain chemical involved in that kind of happiness 'hit' is dopamine, and interestingly this hormone surges *before* we get what we want and then it drops away. When we are *about* to have the bite of cake, or when we're getting ready for the party, we are caught up in the excitement of the chase, and when we actually eat the cake the dopamine drops away; and so our lives are about anticipation. Animals get a big dopamine hit when they think they are about to get fed; 'about to happen' is always the exciting part. 'When I am rich'; 'When I meet the right person'; 'When I achieve the body I want'. . . . We never actually get there, as the anticipation leads to a habit of looking for the next thing, which means we never feel we truly arrive. There is always an 'if', 'when' or 'because' to our happiness.

TRUE, ENDURING HAPPINESS

A myth we have believed throughout our lives is that we have to 'get' happiness, and if we can just get the external details of our lives right, we will be happy. This is not happiness, it is a form of enslavement.

We seem to assume that happiness, and suffering too, come *to* us from 'outside'. Surely, however, it is our thoughts and reactions which are the real defining factors. Furthermore, if it's the case that two or more people don't always find that the same things make them happy or unhappy, then it means we are talking about a mental experience within us, not the things around us.

This book is about turning within and finding the

source of happiness that lies inside us. Rather than being a random feeling we might be lucky enough to experience, I think happiness is a *skill* we can learn; I see it as a product of mental training, and I believe we are hard-wired for it at a deep level. Through learning meditation and mindfulness, we can *choose* to be happy, *no matter what*. Without these tools, we may constantly find ourselves victims of what might or might not happen.

Of course, there are many people in this world going through extremely harsh times, where even the possibility of happiness seems incredibly remote. Perhaps all someone can do is try to survive, but once they have breathing space, meditation can provide them with powerful protection for when they are next in difficulty. This builds a mental resilience that can enable a person to get through even the most difficult situations.

HAPPINESS IS FREEDOM

What does happiness *feel* like? We are completely in the present, with no urge to hang on to the past or ruminate about the future; we are right here in the moment, feeling complete. There is a sense of *freedom*; when we are genuinely happy, we are free from desire and other conflicting emotions. We are free from *wanting* happiness. When we are *searching* for that happiness, there is a sense of hunger, of incompleteness; we are wrapped up in the expectation of getting what we want and the fear of not getting it; we feel trapped by uncertainty. We think we can only be happy when our goals are completed, which means that life is always about the future rather than the present moment.

Normally our minds don't feel free. Thoughts and emotions create a storm inside us, and we easily become their slaves. Moment to moment we might find ourselves in an 'argument' with reality, constantly wishing things were different. Happiness involves mastering our thoughts and emotions and embracing things just as they are; it means that we relax and stop trying to manipulate our circumstances. If we can learn how to rest deeply in the present moment, even when facing difficulties, and we train our minds not to judge, we can discover within us a tremendous source of happiness and satisfaction. We might start to notice how much we usually look for nourishment from 'outer' things instead.

If we imagine someone in a perfect situation where they feel completely happy, and we examine what they are feeling, we can identify a state of mind where 'complete' is the crucial term. That person has *freedom*. Those feelings of completeness, peace, no more striving, no fear, are mental states. As we've seen, we normally think 'things' will make us happy, but if it's an experience of the mind, why not simply 'cut out the middleman' and go straight for the actual happiness?

MEDITATION AND HAPPINESS

I wrote this book because I am passionate about helping people realise they can *choose happiness*, and I wanted to show how this can be learned through the power of meditation. Meditation helps us to access what feels like a deep well within, filled with nourishing water that we can drink whenever we want.

Instead of feeling as if our lives are spinning out of control, with stress, loneliness and dissatisfaction dominating our minds, we can become more connected within, more centred, even in busy situations. Our happiness and our problems both depend upon our state of mind, yet most of us go through life with very little insight into the mind and its true potential. If we are to make some sense of this world, we urgently need to understand our own minds. Meditation and mindfulness are powerful tools for a complete internal revolution.

MYTHS ABOUT MEDITATION

There are several misconceptions about meditation and mindfulness, which I hope this book will help to clarify.

'I would love to meditate but my mind is too busy.'

Many people think that meditation is about stilling or quieting the mind, and they feel their minds are too active and busy to even try. But the *amount* of thoughts we have makes no difference to our meditation; it's not about clearing or blanking out the mind, or going into a trance – that will simply not work and has no real value. Meditation changes our relationship with our thoughts and emotions; it is not aimed at getting rid of them.

Some view meditation as a form of escapism, with very little to do with their busy lives. Or they simply see it as a way to reduce stress and to keep sadness at bay, like dieting or going to the gym to keep their weight under control. Some even feel that meditation is a totally selfish enterprise. These myths are perhaps based on lack of information or incorrect assumptions. Meditation is not a spa treatment: it is a way to connect with our essence and to become who we truly are. Mindfulness is how to bring that awareness into every situation. Our consciousness is the key to everything, and it now feels that the growth of interest in mindfulness in our culture reflects a new step in human evolution: life forms evolve in response to their environment, and it seems our pressurised world is now pushing us to meditate for survival.

I too now have a smartphone and I travel for around 300 days per year. I'm very much embedded in the fast pace of life, and if I didn't meditate every day, I don't know how I would manage. But more than that, meditation has helped me to understand something about happiness.

The aim of this book is to help you create happiness through bringing meditation into the heart of your daily life – not only to reduce stress and gain greater mastery over your thoughts and emotions, but also to discover your mind's deep potential for unconditional compassion and freedom. Happiness is inside you, waiting.

CHAPTER TWO

Hard-wired to be Happy

• • •

According to Buddhist philosophy, we are programmed at a deep level for happiness; it is in our 'hard drive'. The very reason we can be happy is because it is our true nature. This is why we feel things are in their rightful state when we're happy; suffering feels like an intrusion into how things should be. Ultimately we are more than our problems and our pain, and perhaps the fact that you have picked up this book suggests that deep down you have a feeling you are able to tap into the happiness that lies within you.

* * *

FREEDOM WITHIN

As we saw in Chapter One, genuine happiness is really a state of freedom. Being free is the one thing we humans care about most – we don't want to be controlled by others, and we know that we deserve the freedom to do or be whatever we want; this is something we fight hard for, and as a society we have won some important battles. We live in a world of choices, where in many (unfortunately not all) areas of the world, we can dress, speak and think however we want. It's a 'free society', but are we ever *truly* free? We'd like to think we are 'freethinking' individuals, but our minds are not really that free at all.

Where is the freedom when our minds go to places we *don't* want, and don't do what we want? We become enslaved by thoughts and feelings over which we seem to have very little control. We get lost in a mood, painful memories or worries about the future; we would really rather let these things go, but we don't know how to stop thinking about them. We find it hard to sustain focus as our minds constantly drift here and there, sometimes stuck in uncomfortable feelings. It often feels as if we are not really behind the wheel of the car, with our minds going all over the place.

However, it is important to note that we don't experience any of these thoughts or emotions 100 per cent of the time; there is an ever-changing flow, in fact many thousands of changes per day. From the point of view of meditation, this is encouraging, as we can learn methods which help us consciously direct this flow. Our thoughts and emotions are really just habits, and so we can build new, positive ones and become less habituated to those that are negative.

Scientists have recently coined the term 'neuroplasticity' to describe this phenomenon, which simply means the potential for mental change through training, such as meditation, leading to the creation of new neural pathways. We can imprint a multitude of new habits, unlearn negative ones and achieve lasting benefits.

Personally, I've found that some of the most painful and destructive habits I used to suffer from have radically changed through meditation training. I used to experience extreme levels of self-hatred, for example, and this has pretty much gone away. I have also found it incredibly transformative to see that we can step back and observe what our minds are doing. I am learning how not to drown so much in that whirlpool of mental activity, and to find some space behind it all. If we can discover that our minds are bigger than our problems, we'll see that deep down we all have the potential to be truly happy.

THE OBSERVER

I find it fascinating that we can observe our thoughts and emotions. As we go through our day, whenever we are angry, afraid or sad, for example, we usually *know* that we are angry, afraid or sad – we are experiencing how we feel. But if there is a part of the mind that *knows* we are angry, then surely that part is *not* angry – otherwise, how could it know the anger? And so there is an aspect of the mind that is always free.

When we are suffering (feeling emotional pain and facing difficulties) we usually completely identify with that painful state of mind; it becomes our entire reality. When we practise meditation, however, we can learn to identify with the part of the mind which observes that emotion; we can discover that the backdrop of all experiences is spacious and free. That *awareness* is far greater than the pain and suffering we so often find ourselves caught up in.

In ancient texts on meditation one often finds metaphors in which the mind is compared to the sky, and our thoughts and emotions to the clouds. The sky is limitless, vast and without centre or edges. Within the sky there are all kinds of clouds – heavy storm clouds, cotton-wool-like clouds, thin, wispy cirrus clouds and so on. These are all a natural part of the sky, but the sky is bigger. In a similar way, meditation teachings describe the pristine openness and spaciousness of the mind's awareness, which is greater than the comings and goings of the thoughts and emotions.

Our major problem is that we don't *recognise* that awareness. We are lost in our thoughts and emotions; we're lost in the clouds. Meditation helps us to connect with awareness, and it is not about getting rid of the thoughts, but about gaining a broader perspective. The fact that there is this part of the mind which can observe, suggests that our essence is freedom. And as we now know: *freedom is happiness.*

I think many people see meditation as simply a way to reduce stress, but it is actually a method for connecting with our essence, which is complete freedom and happiness. One of the Tibetan words for meditation is '*gom*', which literally means 'to become familiar with', and so we are making friends with our awareness, that ability to observe.

My meditation teacher often used to advise me to stop taking myself so seriously, and what he meant was to stop clinging to those clouds. They are not solid objects. Imagine you're in an aeroplane; as you look out of the window, you see the clouds below you, looking like dense cotton wool, thick and solid. As the plane comes down to land, a child might think the plane will crash into those clouds, but of course we know that despite their appearance, they're insubstantial. Similarly, as we experience our thoughts and emotions, we usually tense up in a kind of fear that we will crash into them, because we think of them as real, and so we react. Relating to our thoughts and emotions in this way is why we suffer.

We usually feel as if thoughts and emotions are coming *into* our heads. We often use the phrase 'something popped into my head'. From where? Are we downloading thoughts and feelings from a virtual hard drive somewhere? Of course not. To explore how mental activity arises, we can consider another metaphor often used to portray the mind – where the mind is compared to the ocean. The ocean represents the mind, and the waves the thoughts and emotions. The ocean's waves are an integral part of it, they come and they go. We could learn to leave things alone and rest in the awareness – the ocean – rather than being thrown around by the waves. This is what meditation practice is all about. When a wave rises in the ocean, does it separate off from the rest of the water and hang in mid-air? No, the wave is just the natural expression of the ocean, and in the same way our thoughts and feelings are simply part of the mind. If we could 'be' the awareness, like 'being' the ocean, life would feel very different. Otherwise, we fall prey to the tossing of the waves and find ourselves controlled by whatever's happening in our minds.

OUR ESSENCE IS FREE

The heart is luminous, but it is obscured by veils which are not of its nature.

– Buddha

The essence of the mind is sometimes described in meditation texts as being like a crystal covered by layers of mud. No matter how thick the mud, the crystal is always there. The mud simply represents the stains of our negative thoughts and emotions. Through meditation, we can wash away the mud so that our crystal can shine.

If deep down, the mind is more than just its thoughts and emotions, this signifies freedom, which is complete happiness. As we gain familiarity with that, we might begin to discover that the mind is essentially *good* – underneath all of our problems we are okay. That is the meaning of *Buddha*. Buddha means *basic innate goodness*, the purity within us.

THE SCIENCE OF THE MIND

Our deep potential for happiness and freedom also exists at a physical level. It is no longer seen as a mystical belief, but is being discussed within neuroscience; it is now regarded as neurological fact. The work of late neuroscientist Candace Pert was particularly interesting in this field. Pert was the pioneer who discovered opioid receptors and endorphins (the body's natural chemicals used to free us from pain), which led her to famously state: 'We are hard-wired for bliss.' Our natural state is to feel good – we are built for happiness.

I frequently collaborate with Yale neuroscientist Ash Ranpura, who describes how when things are going well, the brain simply ticks over in its default state, but if we are about to trip and fall, for example, it generates an 'error signal' which kicks into gear. I find it interesting that our brains are programmed to notice what's wrong, not what's right. To me, this points to the fact that our natural state is positive; we only need to pay attention when we are in danger of moving away from that state. Simply put, when we are walking in a park on a glorious sunny day, and we have a toothache, we take the sunshine and beauty for granted, but tend to focus on the painful tooth. We are primed to notice what's wrong, as it feels like an intrusion into our natural state.

As babies, when we are placed on our mother's body and she feeds us, both mother and child are filled with the natural chemistry of happiness, love and security, which is called oxytocin, and this puts us back into the calm state where we feel most natural. We cry when we are separated from that happiness. We all have a natural biology of contentment, which our bodies know how to generate; when we move away from that state, our bodies are programmed to re-establish it.

This may sound counter-intuitive, but any time we feel a negative emotion, it can actually be seen as proof that our true potential for happiness is limitless. What I mean by this is that when a negative emotion arises, it's because we are in some way feeling frustrated and are looking for something that will make us feel better. The reality, however, is that *nothing* will be good enough for us, as our desire is boundless. Instead, what we need to do is tap into the *true* happiness which is only possible when we are in harmony with our real potential for freedom.

Nothing in this world can ever match the 'hard-wired bliss' which is within us.

What stops us from experiencing that true happiness? It is our tendency to *grasp* at things, even at our thoughts and emotions. This propels us into suffering and stress. We are too focused on seeking happiness and a sense of feeling complete, by searching in the outside world. What we can learn through meditation is that this wholeness has been within us all the time: deep down we have always been completely free and happy.

CHAPTER THREE

Stress in the 21st Century

● ● ●

I became a monk in 1993, at the age of 21. Nobody, least of all myself, could ever have pictured me in a monastery.

I grew up in the South of England and received an incredible education at the University of Oxford. I had been a musician and was now an actor. I lived in New York and had a lovely apartment in Greenwich Village. I only used my kitchen once – to make popcorn when I was throwing a party; the rest of the time I was out on the town. I had a lot of money and was surrounded by friends. I wore the most fashionable clothes and was the life of every party, but I was damaged. In fact, I was completely off the rails.

I lived an extremely wild life, consumed by many addictions, which led me to a number of dangerous situations in which I could easily have lost my life. I was ambitious, and my mind ran at great speed, always searching for something; I was very far from happy and was burning myself out physically and mentally. I remember feeling constantly afraid of my own mind, so I made sure I was never alone. Even walking down the street, I would always have loud music blaring in my headphones, so that I wouldn't have to face my thoughts, and I would imagine myself being somewhere else. I rarely spent the night alone.

I had come to New York to study at a very progressive conservatory on Broadway. In the 'method acting' classes we were shown how to 'use' our past in order to create trauma in ourselves on stage. We would visualise things from past events in order to 'throw' our minds and bodies back into the pain. During one session, I so vividly brought up something quite terrible which had happened in my early teens, that I began to have heart palpitations and a panic attack. Everyone around me was clapping, and I felt as if I was going to die. I suppose I was a good actor, but the cost was high.

One morning I woke up after a heavy night of partying, thinking I was having a heart attack. My heart was beating incredibly fast, I had chest pains and was bathed in sweat. It was hard to move. This led to a long and severe phase of sickness, during which I was bedridden for several months with doctors telling me I had suffered a serious burnout due to stress and excessive living. I had atrial fibrillation – a heart condition that can become dangerous. I was terrified and felt that my life was over.

I moved in with my mother, who was also living in the States. She looked after me, and as I scrabbled around for answers she gave me some books on meditation. My best friend from childhood told me about a Tibetan Buddhist monastery in Scotland that had recently opened its doors to people who wanted to become monks and nuns for a year, and she suggested we go there together. This seemed like a somewhat crazy idea, but it also felt completely right; I decided it was exactly what I needed to do.

I managed to get my health stable enough to travel back to the UK, but I was still incredibly fragile; I vividly remember a horrible panic attack I had in a video store just before I joined the monastery. I suddenly became short of breath and had to sit down on the floor, consumed with a nameless fear. I had the overwhelming feeling that the video boxes were going to jump off the shelves to assault me. The attack passed after a few minutes, but it was terrifying and from that time until quite a few years later, I had recurrent bouts of anxiety and also depression, sometimes extreme.

And so, in 1993 I became a Buddhist monk. All my friends were shocked, as I was not at all 'monk material'. I had always been the party animal, and the most materialistic of my friends. I remember a friend at college had joined a meditation group, and she would often try to drag me along with her, but I would refuse and tell her I'd meet her for a drink afterwards. Maybe I was afraid of my own mind.

I have in fact spent many years driven by fear; I now understand that this mental tendency is rooted in grasping. It can be argued that grasping lies at the heart of all our problems.

GRASPING

We can define grasping as our tendency to grab at things in the world around us, and also how the mind runs after thoughts and emotions. Additionally, we have a habit of *pushing away* discomfort and those thoughts and emotions that we don't like; the rejection is just another form of grasping.

We live with a constant feeling of racing towards something, but we're not quite sure what that thing is. We go to bed at night and the next morning we get up and start rushing again. Where is this heading? What's the overall aim or purpose? Survival, putting food on the table, success, enjoyment, love . . . But for what?

The CEO, the prisoner, the busy parent, the monk – we are all seeking the same thing: happiness and the absence of pain or discomfort. That search for happiness leads us to latch on to things: we look around us and decide what it is we need to be happy. We are all materialistic in different ways, whether it's shopping, dinner with friends or a walk in nature, we grab on to the 'material' around us. Even a beautiful sunset becomes a type of materialism when we externalise and project our happiness onto it. The problem is that when we get something, we pretty soon want something else. That process never stops, as things never seem to be enough. It feels that the things we run after are perpetually elusive, and so there's always something more to search for; and the things we run away from never seem to stop chasing us. This struggle is exhausting; it is what we know as 'stress'.

WHY WE EXPERIENCE STRESS

There are four main factors that lead to stress, and they are all aspects of grasping:

1. Not getting what we want
2. Getting what we *don't* want
3. Protecting what we have
4. Losing what we love

1. Not getting what we want

Do we ever know what we truly want? We think it's 'this' or 'that', but we then discover it was something else. We never actually get what we want, because even if we do, we find we want more of it or we want something different. Advertisers love this about us: we get, and then start searching around for more, or for something else. We think that when we obtain the thing we're chasing, our craving for it will be fulfilled, but just like an addict injecting heroin into their arm, we then need more. The craving simply creates more craving: the habit comes first, not the object, and so we never run out of desire.

Not only is our desire insatiable, but the things we rely on for our happiness are inevitably unsatisfying due to their inability to last forever. Because everything is impermanent, we end up depending on the unreliable. Knowing this creates a subtle undercurrent of uncertainty and insecurity in our minds. Our dependence on the objects and people around us turns us into victims of what might or might not happen. Life seems to be happening *to* us.

We don't know what we want – we think it's something external, but as we learned in the previous chapter, what we *truly* yearn for is *complete and total freedom*. The things we do in the name of that quest don't bring real freedom, they simply create more need – and so there is no lasting fulfilment. Everything feels too limited for us and so nothing will satisfy us except waking up to our ultimate potential – the inner happiness which has no limitations.

2. Getting what we *don't* want

We often get what we *don't* want. We encounter experiences that make us uncomfortable: people, events, places, sensations, etc. Pushing things away, however, simply leads to a habit of needing to push away more and more, and so there will always be something to run away from. We carry a feeling around with us that there's constantly something there to bother us, and in fact every move we make is somehow based on evading discomfort.

3. Protecting what we have

We also experience the pressure of maintenance – holding on to the things we are attached to: people, places, objects, lifestyle, our appearance, etc. But things don't last forever, and so it can feel as if sand is slipping through our fingers: we hold on tight, but the sand keeps pouring through the gaps. Keeping a grip on things and maintaining them is exhausting, and eventually we experience loss.

4. Losing what we love

Nothing lasts. The word 'forever' is a lie, and this impermanence causes us a lot of pain. Even when we're enjoying something, a part of us is already anticipating the sense of loss, and we cannot bear that. Our relationships tend to suffer due to this fear of impermanence, where the anxiety drives people to behave in controlling, even suffocating ways.

In summary, because we don't know how to connect with our inner potential for happiness, we assume that happiness and suffering come from outside. We don't recognise that they are states of mind, and so we grasp in the four ways just described, which leads to stress. Additionally, we are wrapped up in an internal battle: our deepest addiction is to our thoughts and emotions; we see them as real, and we chase, reject and react to them many thousands of times per day, instead of simply leaving them be. We are clinging to the clouds instead of relaxing into the sky (see p. 17), and therefore we don't experience the peace, freedom and happiness which are our true inner nature.

STRESS AND THE BODY

Running after our thoughts all day can make our heads seem like 'spaghetti junction', with our brains feeling burned to a cinder, exhausted. Our stress originates in the way we relate to our thoughts and emotions, and it then manifests in the body, largely due to an over-production of the stress hormone, cortisol.

This hormone is produced as a result of the body's innate 'fight-or-flight' response, which evolved as a survival mechanism: it enabled our ancestors and other mammals to react quickly to life-threatening situations. As hunter-gatherers, we were in danger much of the time – from the elements, large predators and other hunter-gatherers running after us with spears. When danger approached, our bodies would produce cortisol and other hormones to get us into danger mode, ready either to fight – punch a woolly mammoth on the nose – or flee – run away at great speed. Through this survival activity we burned off the cortisol and our levels returned to normal.

We can observe this process today if we look at gazelle or zebra, for example, in Africa. They graze peacefully on the plains, but when a lion approaches, flight mode takes over and they instantly race away. Those that don't get eaten rush to safety and immediately return to grazing; their chemical levels return to normal, they are not traumatised and don't need to hold a meeting to 'unpack' what just happened. They are back to a state of calm, and life goes on. This is the natural response to pressure and danger.

In our 21st century, however, we experience a kind of mini fight-or-flight multiple times per day; our internal technology is still wired for it. If we are walking down a dark street at night that response is, of course, highly useful, as it helps that we are slightly on edge, but when we are sitting behind a desk it is another matter. The amygdala – the part of the brain that creates fight-or-flight – cannot seem to separate real from imagined danger; it simply reacts to pressure, and we can spend our day feeling hunted as we get bombarded with emails.

We don't need to be in danger mode throughout the day; lurching from one cortisol spike to the next is exhausting and toxic. It can damage our organs, contributes to hypertension and diabetes and can influence the way our body distributes its fat. Even a steady trickle of cortisol throughout the day makes us feel tired, as we are not working it off through actual, physical fight or flight. The cortisol causes us to burn up our blood sugar and energy, and we're left depleted. We then grab more chemicals to try to feel better; caffeine and sugar are usually the drugs of choice.

We are exhausted. The huge prevalence of coffee bars in our cities is a relatively recent phenomenon, and now people are reaching for the double or triple shot, like an electric jolt to the heart to get them going again. This is often combined with sugary snacks, and much of today's food is laced with stimulating chemicals which seem to give us an energy lift.

The problem with these drugs is that we get caught in a cycle of increasing exhaustion. We drink coffee to wake up, but we 'borrow from tomorrow' – we are using energy we don't have, and we end up more tired. Then we enter the phase of needing the coffee just to feel normal. It is fascinating how much we are our own chemistry lab, and the question is what are we cooking? For many people that lab is unfortunately more like a 'meth lab' where we throw together masses of toxic chemicals hoping they will make us feel good – but in reality we are simply 'breaking bad'.

MODERN LIVING

Modern life tends to be characterised by an overload of busyness and the stress hormone cortisol. A grasping mentality is exhausting, and the things we surround ourselves with to satisfy that grasping also tend to drain our energy. We can reach the end of our working day and feel as though we've been climbing a mountain or have been dragged through a series of hedges backwards. Our bodies feel wrecked, even though in many cases there hasn't been much physical activity. It is our minds that are worn out.

Nowadays being busy is seen as a mark of success, a badge of honour. We ask each other 'How are you?' and we automatically answer, 'Busy', which means that all is well. We live in a culture of *doing* rather than *being*. Keeping busy is somehow glamorous; it defines us.

Of course, we need to work to pay the bills, support our families and generally contribute to society. But we have constructed a culture in which we are no longer simply growing the food we need to eat and protecting ourselves from danger; we are now locked into a complex matrix of buying, selling, comparing, insuring, communicating and endless growth. This system has become exhausting to maintain, the planet is unable to sustain our demands and meanwhile we run around our cities, busy all day keeping the system running. We validate ourselves through this achievement.

The real problem is that we are out of touch with the true beauty of our own minds, as described in Chapter Two, and so we become obsessed with an identity based on a veneer of external achievements. As a society, we learn to believe that we don't have actual value in and of ourselves, and so we must obtain that value from outside.

This quest for happiness from external things has not actually made us happy – depression, substance abuse and suicide are at an all-time high in the 'developed' world. So why do we do it? We are wired, since our days as hunter-gatherers, to worry about scarcity. The modern hunter-gatherer can be seen wandering the shopping mall or behind the laptop making online purchases. Many of the things we grasp at provide an instant hit of gratification, and are thus addictive, and the adverts which constantly invade our screens promise more of that. So we are caught in a cycle.

We created the 'digital age' to simplify things, but we seem to have given ourselves more work and have found ourselves spinning faster in the cycle. Interestingly, we are the 'crossover' generation, pre- and post-technology.

The Internet and smartphones have emerged during our lifetimes, and our brains simply weren't ready to catch up. We seem to be forever mentally running behind the latest upgrade. The more advanced our society becomes, the more stress exists.

I was standing on a train recently. Looking up and down the carriage I was struck by how everyone had their faces buried in phone screens; not one of them seemed to notice the beautiful view passing by the windows, and they were probably spiking their cortisol levels by reading their news feeds.

> *The people will not revolt. They will not look up from their screens long enough to notice what's happening.*
>
> – Robert Icke and Duncan Macmillan, stage adaptation of George Orwell's *1984*

This fascinating quote has been circulating on social media for a while, and in true 'alternative facts' style it has been attributed to Orwell himself, when actually it was written in 2013 for a stage adaptation of his book. The irony is that the people reading the quote (on their screens) are being told it was written in 1949, which they believe and then repost. It has now gone viral.

Aside from this interesting glitch, the statement itself is powerful and does seem to characterise modern life. We have found a compelling way to ignore each other (faces buried in screens), to get away from our own thoughts, to consume huge amounts of untruths and to live in a state of constant comparison with other people's lives.

In *1984*, Orwell's novel about a dystopian future, the authorities promote something called 'Newspeak', which Orwell describes as a type of language designed to constrict people's way of thinking and to control how they communicate. This reminds me of how many people interact with Twitter, where all expression is limited to the required 140 (or now 280) characters, which has in some ways led to a society of truncated thinking, experiencing life through 'hashtags', boiling everything down to 'posts'.

Until the Internet age, we were comparing ourselves with the person next door, but now we are looking in minute detail at the lives of Hollywood stars across the planet from us. Envy seems to be the order of the day: magazines love to show photos of famous people with a pimple on their chin, circled in red with an arrow and the caption 'What *were* they thinking?' – the idea being to bring them down, topple them from their pedestals, while at the same time secretly wishing we had their lives.

Teenagers are viewing photos which make them feel

they are not good enough, and are consequently growing up with poor self-image. They often don't realise that much of what people post online is not the real truth, it's a glamourised, filtered version of their lives which they present for other people to 'like'. Models and celebrities appear in airbrushed photos; nobody actually looks like that, but when people see the pictures they can feel an increasing sense of despair that they cannot keep up. A friend told me she was having tea at a fancy London restaurant; two girls at the next table ordered a stack of very ornate pink cakes on silver plates, took photos of themselves with the cakes and then left without eating them. People become addicted to 'likes' on social media, and easily get wrapped up in jealousy and competition. We are losing the ability to know what we like; we have to check if other people 'like' it first.

This outlook on modern living sounds like a rather grim viewpoint, and of course it isn't always so stark. Life can feel great, things can go really well, but we still lack certainty. There is always something that's never quite right, or something good or bad that's *about to* happen. We move through life driven by distraction and stress, assuming that if we can just win the race or battle, we'll be home and dry.

The good news is that meditation can provide a highly effective solution to this problem, helping us to master our thoughts and emotions. Brain scans have even shown that meditation gets the amygdala under control and reduces the overproduction of cortisol.

I have, however, encountered many misconceptions about how meditation works. When I first began to teach in the late 1990s, the mindfulness trend had not yet become popular, and people had less knowledge of its benefits. Some had concerns that practising the techniques would take away their drive, that they would become 'too' relaxed. People often feel they 'need' their stress. When I myself started to meditate I too was worried I might lose my sparkle and end up flat and grey. But instead I've discovered that meditation can create a joy and energy which feel fresh and alive, where you can in fact get more done. We can still be passionate about life and have goals, but we need a bedrock of equanimity so that we can retain a sense of resilience. What we need more than anything is to understand that happiness comes from within.

Being able to produce our own happiness is a life-changing skill, and the next chapter describes this journey.

CHAPTER FOUR

Meditation and Mindfulness

● ● ●

We have an average of between 60,000 and 80,000 thoughts per day. The majority of them aren't that useful, many are repeats and quite a few are negative, however it is futile to try to get rid of them.

There's an old Tibetan saying:

*When you run after your thoughts, you're like a
    dog running after a stick.
But if you throw a stick for a lion, he turns around
    and looks at who threw it.
You only throw a stick at a lion one time.
Be like the lion.*

How we react to our thoughts is what tends to make us unhappy. Meditation turns us into the lion and we can become the 'king of the jungle' of our minds. Only when we get in charge of our thoughts can we really choose to be happy.

Is there a difference between meditation and mindfulness? In modern times meditation has in some ways been 'rebranded' as mindfulness, to make it more accessible. But from a deeper perspective, they are in fact two important aspects of one system of training.

Meditation is where we sit down to train our minds, using specific techniques. *Mindfulness* is how we bring our minds back from distraction during the meditation session, and it also refers to the integration of meditation into daily life. This is done by practising moments of awareness as we go about our activities.

WHAT MEDITATION IS NOT

Many people are attracted to meditation out of a deep urge to 'switch off'. They seek relief from the incessant busyness of their minds, and so they assume the only alternative is total mental silence. This is perfectly understandable; we all have too much going on in our minds – we'd love to get some space from it all, and so we want to 'clear the mind', blank out our thoughts. In reality, that's more like being in a coma or under anaesthesia, and meditating with that aim will simply lead to more stress: 'I can't stop my thoughts. I can't clear my mind. I can't switch off, it's going wrong. I'm just filled with thoughts.' We begin to feel like a failure and many people give up meditating because of this: 'I can't do meditation because I have a very busy mind' or, 'I tried meditation, but it didn't work.'

It is worth questioning how experiencing a blank, empty mind for 10 minutes would provide any benefit to the rest of our busy lives. That's just like being knocked out for a short while. If we think meditation is about having no thoughts, there are much easier ways to achieve that – we could throw ourselves down the stairs and then we'd be unconscious!

The more we try to force our thoughts away, the louder they seem to shout. If you press your hand down on to a spring, it pushes back with equal pressure; if you force a child to sit still, they will fidget and want to move. If you put restrictions on your mind, that mind will stage a revolution.

Several years ago I was invited on to a television programme to talk about meditation. As the technicians were attaching the microphone to my shirt, the producer informed me it was actually going to be a debate about the subject, and my 'opponent' was an Oxford professor who believed that meditation is bad for us. The gentleman looked rather ferocious, and he very forcefully insisted that meditation is highly dangerous. He said, 'We shouldn't be blanking out our minds, we should be *using* them. We need to think, and we need to feel.' I completely agreed with him and there was actually nothing to debate.

It saddens me that so many people think of meditation as the mental version of trying to hold one's breath and suffocate. Meditating like that will simply produce more cortisol, as the brain goes into fight-or-flight mode every time a thought arises.

HOW TO DEAL WITH THOUGHTS

The aim of meditation is *not* to get rid of our thoughts, but to change our relationship with them. 'Inner peace' means to end the war with our thoughts, it certainly doesn't mean to go blank. Can we be 'at peace' with our thoughts, and also with our emotions? This is really the only way to find true happiness, as then we are no longer battling with ourselves.

Meditation is about giving our minds complete freedom; it enables us to find space *within*, rather than *from*, the thoughts. If there are lots of thoughts, that's fine, but we can learn not to be bothered by them, not to get entrapped by them. We can let the mind *be* and leave the thoughts alone. This is difficult for somebody just beginning at meditation, so we can use a focus, such as our breathing, to anchor our attention. We just need to come back to concentrating on the breath when we realise we got carried away by thoughts.

It doesn't matter what kind of thoughts you have during your meditation session – deep sadness or which pizza topping you prefer – they are the same, both are simply mental activity. The key point is that you are developing an awareness of the thoughts and breaking your addiction to them, by bringing your focus back to your breathing, for example. This ultimately means you will get less carried away by your thoughts and emotions. Training in this manner will have a significant beneficial effect on the rest of your life, as even if during the meditation session you're simply letting go of 'I wonder what's for lunch', you're learning something that will protect you from all kinds of stress – the ability to not get caught up. This builds resilience, which means you can become less controlled by unhelpful mental activity. Lifting weights at the gym produces stronger muscles, and you take those muscles with you wherever you go. Similarly, when you train in the mental exercise of not getting dragged around by your thoughts, your mind will become less liable to get lost in negativity.

Meditation is a bit like standing beside a busy road; the road represents our mind and the cars our thoughts and feelings. If we try to stop the cars, they'll pile up and there will be a crash. Instead we could stand at the side of the road and just watch the cars go by. Maybe some of those cars are taxis; if we put our hand out, a taxi stops for us, we get in and go for a drive. That's what we tend to do with our thoughts and feelings: we get into them, just like getting into a taxi, and we go for a long drive around town, without really knowing where we're going, and at the end there's a large bill to pay.

However, we can train ourselves to stand back, simply staying in one spot – which is like using a meditation focus such as the breath, letting those taxis go by.

Meditation is to *let the mind, with its thoughts and emotions, be,* but also to have *awareness.* If we develop that, then it doesn't matter what the thoughts are doing. The awareness is not caught up in the mental activity.

You're like a house,
Leave the front door and back door open,
Allow your thoughts to come and go.
Just don't serve them tea.

– Shunryu Suzuki, Zen Master

As we learned in Chapter Two, the mind is like the sky or the ocean; the sky contains clouds, and the ocean has waves. Neither the sky nor the ocean grab on to their clouds or waves – these are simply part of their natural ebb and flow. The clouds and waves symbolise our mental activity – the thoughts and emotions. Our tendency is either to chase after them or try to get rid of them, but instead we could simply learn to leave them alone. Eventually we might begin to understand that just like the clouds and waves, thoughts and emotions aren't solid after all.

Usually when we experience our thoughts, we strongly *believe* them, and when we encounter emotions – such as anger, sadness or fear – we feel as if there's something very heavy inside us, which we have to do something about. We want to escape from these things, so we either express or repress them, throw them out or push them down, or we wish someone else would come along and take them all away for us. The approach in meditation is to understand that the experience is not actually solid and so we don't need to *do* anything about it; we just need to step back and observe. Our awareness is *not* the thought or the emotion and is free from any suffering. When the meditator reaches that stage, they no longer need to use the breath or other focusing techniques, but can simply rest in the present awareness and not get caught up in the flow of mental activity.

Through this process, we may slowly start to understand that we are actually fundamentally *good*; underneath all of our problems we are okay. Through meditation we could eventually begin to feel our inner potential, that basic goodness within us. That is freedom. That is happiness.

TRANSFORMING NEGATIVITY

The part of us which very often baffles and confuses us is our emotional life – it seems to run the show. We certainly don't *plan* our emotions – we don't decide to have or not to have them; they seem to come from nowhere, and when they are negative, they can be highly detrimental to our happiness. Meditation is not about getting rid of our emotions. Some people worry that meditating might turn them into lifeless robots with no feelings, but the aim is in fact to become more emotionally intelligent, which involves becoming more comfortable with our emotions, less driven by them. But first we need to make friends with a part of ourselves that we have often felt a little afraid of.

Emotions are actually our good friends, as they are in many ways more 'truthful' than thoughts; our thoughts can go around in circles playing all sorts of tricks on us, but how we feel is something we can experience quite viscerally. We often feel emotion in our bodies, and that can represent some kind of truth about who we are in this moment. The problem arises when we react negatively to this, and when our emotions *run* us and make us (and others) suffer.

Negative emotions arise from three major 'afflictive' habits of the mind: craving, anger and confusion. These form the basis for all of our unpleasant emotional experiences such as jealousy, fear, worry and a whole range of other upsetting feelings.

Craving

Craving can also be called grasping. As we've seen, we live in a culture of desire, where we are conditioned to want things, people and experiences, because most people believe that's how one 'gets' happiness. Problems arise when our desire leads to frustration, which is actually 100 per cent of the time – something which advertisers get really excited about.

Wanting implies that we don't have. If we break this down, we can see how the wanting mind becomes a habitual pattern, where we are always wanting something; the wanting itself suggests a sense of lack, and that too grows as a habit, becoming a default state. The more we think 'I want x or y', the more we feel the pain of lacking x or y. Happiness, however, is in fact simply a mind state. If we have x or y, what are we actually feeling? If we are walking in a park in the sunshine, what do we feel in that moment? The feeling occurs in the mind. Through meditation, then, we can learn how to cultivate happiness independently.

Are we talking about a life without desire? Maybe not; perhaps the aim is to be less driven by endless need, and instead to find peace and contentment. Would that stop progress? Will our society collapse? Will people stop going to work or seeking promotions? Absolutely not. It is all about balance. We can still strive for a better life, but we can become less frightened about things working or not working out for us. If we can learn how to produce our own happiness, then anything else is a bonus.

Anger

Anger is interesting; it has so many different layers. Sometimes we experience strong rage, which can feel hot or cold. Hot anger feels like we are burning; it can be a sharp stab in the heart area, or an inflamed sensation rising in our entire body. Cold anger is where we shut down and become icy; we 'stare daggers'. Both are painful, and both cause trouble in our lives and for those around us.

Another aspect of anger is aversion, which is a form of rejection or pushing away. Aversion comes from fear, and it can arise in relation to absolutely anything – people, places, situations, mental or physical sensations, sounds, smells, tastes, mind states . . . *anything*, and it can even be just a mild irritation. But is it the thing itself, or is it actually the habit of mental aversion which is the problem for us? Once we understand the workings of our minds, we can begin to free ourselves.

Just like craving, aversion simply leads to more aversion. The mind which is conditioned to push something away will always find something that needs to be pushed away. Aversion is a habit that constantly seeks someone or something to blame.

Again, would a world without anger mean that nothing gets done? Would injustice go unchecked? Actually, I think greater change comes about when a movement is motivated by compassion, but more on that later.

Confusion

Our biggest confusion is that we think happiness and suffering come from outside, and we don't know our own minds. In general, we don't actually see how confused we are. That is the nature of ignorance: if we don't know, we simply don't know – if we *know* that we don't know, then we are not confused! Confusion about life, about ourselves, about others: these are the real reasons why we don't seem to find lasting happiness or know how to avoid suffering; and so confusion lies at the root of all our emotions.

Our confusion also means that we tend to view the world through a lens that is highly conditioned by our habits and our history. We usually don't see things as they truly are.

Due to these three basic habits – craving, anger and confusion – we experience a plethora of emotions. Most negative emotions arise out of a combination of those three. For example, if we are anxious, it is a mixture of being attached to one particular outcome and feeling aversion towards another, as well as not knowing the true nature of things. On top of this, our minds compulsively hold on to the anxiety: we are locked in to that anxious state, yet at the same time we feel strong aversion towards the feeling – we can't stand it and we want it to go away – and we can't seem to get ourselves out of that state, as we don't know how (confusion); and so we suffer.

Meditation teaches us how to get less wrapped up in these habits. We will still feel our emotions, but we can become less driven and controlled by them.

The shortcut to happiness is to completely change our relationship with our thoughts and emotions. We are often helplessly addicted to them, and meditation helps to cure that addiction. Every time our minds wander and we return to the breath, for example, we are freeing ourselves from our habit of grasping and latching on to our mental activity, and thus we will become less controlled by negativity.

KEY INGREDIENTS FOR MEDITATION

Meditation is practised by setting aside a short period of time to sit down in a quiet place, preferably each day; the next chapter will provide practical advice on this.

The most important thing is to have clear instruction in the techniques. This book aims to help you with that, but you could also find a class and meet good teachers if you have further questions.

The first meditation technique which many people learn is to focus on the body. Because the body is so tangible, this makes it an easy place to start. Another technique, often learned after the body, is to focus on the breathing, thus moving to something more subtle, a little more challenging. There are many other methods, several of which employ the senses, such as listening to sound (whatever noises are naturally there) or looking at a visual object. The key point is that these are all known as meditation 'supports', as they provide a focus for our attention, and when the mind wanders they are a place to return to. We are training in mental focus, and also in coming back to the support when we realise we have got distracted, thus learning how not to get entangled in our thoughts and emotions. As described earlier, when the meditator becomes more experienced, they will no longer need to use the support of one of their senses, but can instead simply rest in their own awareness.

Before getting started it is helpful to understand that a meditation session consists of **THREE PHASES** which are repeated again and again:

THE FIRST PHASE is when we're *fully focused* on the breath (for example). This is where we are concentrated on our breathing and are not wrapped up in our thoughts; we are fully present. Many people think 'Oh, *that's* meditation', but perhaps they don't know about the other two phases.

THE SECOND PHASE is when we *notice* that our minds have wandered. The interesting thing is that we don't see the mind step away from the breath and drift off into thoughts; it's more that after a while we suddenly 'wake up' in our thoughts and realise that we've gone somewhere else. This is the noticing. We are recognising that we got lost, but have now found our awareness again. Many people see this as a moment of failure, but actually it is one of success: we were lost in our thoughts, but now we are aware again. This is mindfulness, and so instead of feeling bad about it, we could feel positive. That quality of joyful enthusiasm is an important part of the training. Rather than letting things become grim and severe, we could joyfully notice that the mind got lost but now we've found it again. It's as if we had lost a precious diamond ring but have now retrieved it – we wouldn't need to dwell on thoughts such as, 'I'm so terrible, I'm always losing rings. I'm dreadful and I should be locked up.' Instead we're over the moon that we have found it again.

THE THIRD PHASE is *returning* our attention to focusing on the breath. We noticed that we got lost, and now we are gently returning to the breath, in a relaxed way.

A meditation session is a constant process of those three things: sometimes we're with the breath, sometimes we're noticing that our minds had got lost in thoughts, and sometimes we're returning to the breath. All three phases are important, as they are different aspects of mindfulness, all of which strengthen us. Training in this manner enables progress, as we become better at noticing more quickly that we got distracted.

If you understand that each of these three phases has great value, it will completely revolutionise your practice, otherwise you might end up feeling like a failure every time your mind wanders. For many people meditation sessions can be tough and frustrating; sitting down to meditate feels like strapping on a suit of armour to go into battle with the mind, having to get the guns out to shoot down the thoughts. Trying to clear the mind means engaging in a fruitless internal war.

With this new understanding, however, we can see that if the point of the practice is to keep returning to the breath, then we actually do need to have somewhere to come back *from*. The wandering mind therefore *helps* us to notice and return, and so it's not a bad thing after all. We no longer need to fight, block or resent our thoughts. The thoughts *aid* our meditation; they are friends rather than enemies, and as we will learn in Chapter Nine (see p. 180), knowing this is the root of compassion.

MEDITATION EXERCISES

The first two exercises in this book provide an introduction to meditation by getting the mind to experience how it normally feels, and then to discover the quality of training our awareness.

As with all the exercises in the book, you could first read through the instructions so that you know what to do, or you could listen to the audio version of the book while doing your session of meditation.

1. Notice the mind

This exercise is about turning your attention inwards, to get a sense of what's happening in your mind.

Sit somewhere comfortable, in a reasonably quiet place. Have a look at what your mind is doing. Notice the thoughts as they come up. Observe how the mind jumps from thought to thought like a monkey swinging between the branches in a forest. The mind is also like a bee or butterfly, flitting around in quite a random manner. Don't try to meditate, just observe.

Simply see what's going on; where is your mind now? Is it in the past? Or in the present? Is it in the future?

Is there a particular mood or emotional state happening within you right now? Or is there a feeling in your body? Explore any sensations you encounter.

It is important to try not to *judge* what you're experiencing. Judgement is where we label things as good or bad, or we try to get rid of them. Simply be aware; see what your mind is doing. Observe the experiences of this moment.

The purpose of this exercise is to notice how active and busy the mind is. Through *seeing* that instability, as well as through reading the meditation advice given in this book, you might develop a natural wish to meditate.

You can also have moments of this throughout your day. From time to time, simply notice what your mind is doing. Observe the thoughts and what kind of mood is present. You could do this many times per day, even when you're busy.

2. Moments of awareness

For this exercise it is best to go somewhere outdoors; perhaps you could sit in the garden or on a bench in a park. If you cannot do that, sit where there's some kind of view, maybe looking through a window. Or if there is no view, just be aware of the room around you.

The exercise is about learning to be present by connecting with your surroundings. Try to do this in a fresh, uncomplicated way; it's like being a child walking through a fairground – that child is completely present and filled with wonder.

If you're outdoors, notice the environment, the grass or the trees. If you are indoors, notice the colours of the view or the room around you. It's as if you're seeing it all for the first time. Drink in the environment, letting your mind fill up with joy as you experience this precious moment.

When you get distracted by thoughts, gently bring your attention back to the freshness of this beautiful present moment. The mind loses contact through drifting away; simply bring back the awareness by refocusing on where you are.

Our problems occur when we are hanging on to the past, worrying about the future or wishing that the present moment were different. In this fresh moment of present awareness, there *are* no problems. All that's needed is to observe, to become aware.

The helpful lesson we can take away from these two initial exercises is that we have experienced the difference between the unsettled and the settled mind. The first exercise showed us how the mind runs all over the place, and the second exercise taught us how to focus and settle into the present moment. Interestingly, both exercises helped us to understand what it means to be aware.

These exercises only need to take a few minutes. In the next chapter we shall go further.

CHAPTER FIVE
Getting Started

• • •

My own start on the meditation journey was quite extreme, joining a monastery after almost having a heart attack through out-of-control stress levels and a life of excess.

I arrived at Kagyu Samye Ling Monastery in Scotland at the age of 21. I tried to tell the Abbot my life story but he simply smiled, looked deep into my eyes and asked if I was ready. Four days later I was a monk.

I made friends with the other monks and nuns quickly. I had expected to find a bunch of rather pious people wearing big hoods, their noses buried in prayer books, but what I discovered was completely different. I found myself among inspiring people, some of whom had been desperately wild just like me, who were now seeking a deeper meaning to life.

One of my first monk friends told me he used to steal television sets by simply walking into a shop, picking one up and walking out with it on his shoulder. People were so scared of him that they never tried to stop him; but he was actually a lovely person. After my first week at the monastery, another friend encouraged me to go to evening prayers, telling me that the chanting 'has a great reggae beat'.

Through the guidance of our revolutionary Tibetan Abbot and the profoundly rich Buddhist teachings, we all slowly began to get our heads straightened out. I am sure we were quite a handful, but the Abbot created a compelling and rich space in which we could each find our way. Everyone began to settle down and meditate. As well as learning how to get to grips with our minds, living under the monastic vows had a profound effect on us. Monks and nuns observe rules such as celibacy and avoiding all intoxicants. This might sound like restrictive abstinence, but such vows can in fact be incredibly liberating.

It was certainly tough at the beginning. The first group meditation session I attended was two hours long, and I sat there holding on for dear life, looking intently at the design on the carpet in front of me, thinking that if I just kept staring at that pattern, I wouldn't go mad.

After this rather rocky start I began to learn meditation in a more gradual way, and I settled into life at the monastery, which involved a mixture of work, study and meditation. I had no plans to stay longer than a year, and in fact I found the senior monks and nuns a little strange – the thought of staying for 'life' felt very bizarre. I remember one of the most senior nuns, who is now a great friend of mine, gently telling me I was wearing my robes back to front, to which I crossly replied, 'Yeah, have you got a problem with that?' In those early days I was a bit rough around the edges.

Something changed one month before the end of that year. I was suddenly overcome by a feeling that I was only experiencing the tip of an iceberg. The Buddhist philosophy and the advice of my teachers had started to get under my skin, and I decided to stay longer. I took vows for another year.

When I first met my teacher, the renowned Tibetan master Choje Akong Tulku Rinpoche, I didn't really like him. I thought he was grumpy. I respected him, could see that he was powerful in a good way and was working tirelessly to help people all over the world, but I wanted to stay away from him. I think I was scared of the truth he represented. I would alternate between avoiding him and running to his office to find relief from the anguish of my emotions.

I slowly got to know him. One day when I went to talk to him, I found him walking around a huge circular desk littered with papers – documents relating to his extensive charity projects in some of the world's poorest countries. He was padding around in his socks, in a very relaxed manner, casually eating dry muesli out of a small plastic bag, and I suddenly got the feeling that his mind was as vast as the sky. From that moment on I trusted him completely and wanted to learn everything he could teach me.

Rinpoche began to teach me how to work with my mind. He also guided me into undertaking solitary meditation retreats. In my second year at the monastery I entered my first retreat, spending nine months in isolation. I moved into a secluded house up the hill from the monastery; people were taking bets to see if I would survive, but Rinpoche encouraged me.

Over the course of the retreat I went to quite an extreme, fasting every alternate day and observing silence, while doing long sessions of meditation practice. It was a time when everything was intensified, and I remember feeling confused and yet somehow driven to carry on. The meditations I was practising were based around compassion, and I started to become obsessed with the idea of service, helping others. I thought of becoming a doctor or a nurse, which then developed into a decision to dedicate my life to being a monk. This would mean keeping the vows for my entire life, always wearing the monk's robes, and living a life devoted to meditation training and helping others. I became convinced that such a life would be useful and meaningful, and I realised that if I learned more about meditation, this could enable me to contribute something to others which felt valuable. At the same time the thought of it terrified me, and I wanted to run back to New York. Finally, however, I plunged in and took 'lifelong vows', and as soon as I came out of the vow-taking ceremony I felt every cell in my body click into place. It felt like I had come home. At the time of writing, I have been a monk for 26 years. Soon after I made the commitment, Rinpoche encouraged me to start teaching basic meditation.

BEGIN WITH THE SENSES

As we learned in the previous chapter, we can begin our training by learning to focus our attention on our senses. We could focus on our body, our breathing, listening to sounds or looking at a visual object. This helps us to be present, and it teaches us how not to get too entangled in our thoughts. We train in returning to our chosen focus when we realise our minds have wandered.

Our brains can do many types of multitasking. For example, we can talk to the person next to us while driving a car, but interestingly, we cannot focus on one of our senses and be caught up in thinking simultaneously. Just as it's impossible to drive a car in two gears, we cannot be in a state of stress and one of calm at the same time.

A metaphor for this practice of using the senses is that the mind is like a monkey living inside a house. There are five windows, which represent our five senses. The monkey, which represents our consciousness, rushes around inside and keeps looking out of different windows. If you were standing outside the house, it might appear as if there were five monkeys, because the monkey flits about so fast, its face quickly appearing at each window.

There is also a lot of 'stuff' inside the house; this represents our thoughts and emotions, and sometimes the monkey is busy rummaging through all of that, looking for food.

Meditation is like getting the monkey to look out of just one of those windows and stay there – i.e. focusing on one of our sense 'doorways', instead of jumping about; and so in meditation we might use the feeling of the breath, or we might look at a visual object, or we could use any of our senses.

HOW TO START

To begin, begin.

– William Wordsworth

If you want to learn meditation, it's good to just begin, right now, without hesitating. You don't need to wait until you're 'ready'. In every moment you are ready.

Where to meditate

The ideal place for a meditation session is a quiet area. It doesn't need to be 100 per cent silent, which is impossible to achieve anyway, but it should at least feel relatively quiet. It's best to position yourself where there isn't a huge amount of space or a door or window behind you, otherwise you may feel unsettled, as if you sense something might be behind you. This is a natural reaction, a survival mechanism, as we are hard-wired, just like animals, to protect ourselves by always being on the alert for danger. An ideal position would be with a wall or the corner of the room behind you, providing a sense of security and stability. Make sure the room is not too stuffy or warm, as this can lead to sleepiness.

How to sit

Posture is important, as the mind and body are linked. The traditional position for meditation is to sit cross-legged on the floor, usually sitting off the edge of a small cushion, but many people prefer to sit on a chair, which is fine. The main point is to have a straight back. Rather than leaning against the back of the chair, you could place a small cushion behind the base of your spine, for lower back support, but the rest of your back is upright and unsupported unless you have a physical issue. Sitting upright like this will promote awareness and prevent drowsiness so using quite a firm chair is best. Of course meditation can be done lying down if that is all you can manage.

Your feet are in parallel, flat on the floor, and your hands can be in your lap, resting with the palms up – right hand on top of the left, the tips of the thumbs just touching – or place your hands on your legs, with the palms down on your knees or thighs. These hand positions help to create a sense of symmetry and balance for body and mind.

Your back is straight, and the neck is slightly lengthened by tucking in your chin slightly as if you're making a bit of a double chin. Your face is very relaxed, with the lips and teeth neither clenched shut nor hanging open – there should be just a little space there. Place the tip of your tongue against the roof of the mouth, just behind the top row of teeth (this stops you producing too much distracting saliva).

Eyes open or closed?
It's better if your eyes are open, not looking around the room, but gazing into the space in front of you, perhaps at an angle downwards, and of course you should blink whenever you need to. You're not particularly focusing on anything, you're just looking into space.

Leaving the eyes open means you'll get less drowsy or sleepy, and it also promotes the development of awareness and presence. Also, if you close your eyes to meditate, you could start to associate the meditative state with darkness, and it then becomes much harder to mix your practice into daily life – bringing that meditation into your everyday activities. Maybe you want to close your eyes because you feel the visual objects around you are distractions, impediments to your peace and tranquillity. However, by promoting this mentality, you could be building a subtle sense of fear, through labelling the outer world as the 'enemy' of your mind. In fact, the 'outer' world is simply what is experienced *with* the mind, and so you could simply relax with it instead of needing to shut it down.

Perhaps wanting to close the eyes suggests that we associate meditation with switching off, going 'under', as in a trance or hypnotic state, which points to some of our deeply rooted beliefs around relaxation. People tend to think of relaxation as a passive, switched-off state, whereas meditation cultivates a type of relaxation that contains clarity and awareness. With the eyes open you can develop greater mental clarity rather than sliding into a dull or sleepy state.

Meditating with the eyes open is a statement that everything is fine just as it is, that there is no need to get rid of anything. This creates a sense of openness and fearlessness – the psychology of being 'okay with everything'. You're learning to be present without altering anything, therefore you are *truly* in this moment, just as it is. Many people struggle with this at first, because they have an urge to shut down and escape. But if you persevere, the benefits are tangible.

Music?

Some people like to have background music, or some kind of calming audio track, when they meditate, but this isn't actually a great idea. It creates an association between the meditation and those sounds, which means it will be harder to integrate the practice into daily life, as you will always need the music to enable you to click into the mindful state. Also, the use of music suggests that *you* are not enough – that you need something extra in order to find peace – whereas actually everything you need is within you. You don't need to listen to dolphin noises or sounds of the rainforest. Doing that can simply make you feel more disgruntled with the ordinariness of mundane life, instead of discovering the beauty and simplicity of the unelaborated present moment.

Guided meditation – a vocal track guiding your practice – is not essential, but some people find it useful when learning meditation or a new technique, almost like having a personal trainer for the mind. You could even try using a meditation app. Guidance is not so great, however, when it becomes a 'crutch'; after some time you could grow dependent on the person's voice, which means you're not actually doing the meditation for yourself – your mind wanders and it is the voice, not you, that brings you back to the focus. So it is best to then go 'solo', like taking the stabilisers off a bicycle.

How long for, and when is best?
The ideal length of time for a session depends on how experienced you are. For a beginner it is usually good to start with 10 minutes once or twice a day – this becomes sustainable, as it doesn't feel as if you're forcing your mind too radically. Then you could start to extend the length of your session over time. Eventually a 30-minute session becomes a really stable daily habit and of course longer or multiple sessions per day are even better. It is good to have a baseline timing as a minimum commitment below which you will not drop, as this builds discipline. You will need some kind of timing device, even an alarm (as long as it's a gentle, not shocking sound!). If you sit down and simply decide to 'see how it goes', it becomes harder to instil discipline; you will find yourself giving into restlessness as soon as it feels challenging. So it's best to time the session.

Morning is the ideal time for meditation; it means you're starting your day in the best manner possible, setting the tone for how you wish it to continue. Cortisol levels are highest in the morning – we experience a spike in the hormone to help our body move from the sleep state to the waking state – so it's good to bring the levels back to normal with meditation before starting the day. Many people start their day in quite a hectic manner, 'shocked' awake by an alarm clock. They might throw some coffee down their throats and then rush to work, college or to take the children to school. Maybe you need to use an alarm clock to wake up, but at least you could then bring your cortisol levels into balance before continuing with your day.

Spiritual texts state that the period between the hours of 4am and 7am is the optimal time for spiritual training; it's called the time of 'upward rising energy', as all the flowers are opening; but other times are also fine – for some people the mornings are just impossible, so they meditate later on in the day or in the evening.

Some people find it helpful to set a daily time for meditation, to formally schedule it in, creating a sense of commitment. For others this can become a problem, as if they miss a session that day, they feel they've 'blown it' for the day, and that they'll have to try again tomorrow instead of simply doing the session later in the day. It's therefore important to be skilful in how you handle your own discipline and to find your own best way.

MEDITATION EXERCISES

For beginners it's helpful to start by using the body as the meditation 'focus' – it's easier to concentrate on the body, as the sense of touch is the most tangible of our senses, and it provides an excellent basis for all the other methods of meditation.

As with all the exercises in this book, you could first read through the instructions so that you know what to do, or you could listen to the audio version of the book while doing your session of meditation.

1. Connecting with the body

Sit in a comfortable chair, in a relatively quiet place. For these early exercises it's not essential to sit bolt upright, and so you could use an armchair. We will introduce a more disciplined posture when we learn the later meditations. For now, simply be balanced and comfortable.

Take in the room around you. Your eyes are open but you're not moving your head around too much. Be aware of your surroundings. Explore any particular quality to the light in the room; maybe there are shadows or different textures of light. Listen out for any background noise, or notice any smells. Be present and take it all in, trying not to label things too much.

Next, focus your attention on the feeling of the chair under you; notice the points of contact between your body and the seat.

After a few moments switch your focus to the feeling of the texture of the clothing under your hands, which are resting in your lap or on your legs.

Then feel the ground under your feet. Again, notice the sensation of contact between your feet and the floor.

Become aware of your shoulders; maybe they feel tense or tight, but don't worry about that, just be aware of that area for a few moments, in a neutral way.

Focus on your face. Is there any kind of taste in your mouth? Without moving your mouth around, simply experience what is there, with a light touch of curious observation.

Lastly bring your focus to the front of your body and feel how your breath (breathing naturally) is causing your body to gently contract and expand in a rhythmical manner.

This exercise can be quite short – 5 or 10 minutes.

2. The mindful body

For this deeper exercise you'll be moving your attention up and down your body while maintaining a sense of focus. Many people call this practice the 'body scan'. That name can be helpful, as in some ways it's like an MRI scanner, where there's a neutral observation combined with the steady movement of attention. The meditation involves moving your focus very slowly through the different areas of your body, taking in an entire area at each place. There's a steady line of awareness moving first up, and then down the body, just like a scanner.

You're not trying to feel anything – there may be areas of the body where there's strong sensation, either pain or tension, but there are other areas where you'll feel nothing. It's all the same, you're simply experiencing your body without judgement or labels.

You aren't *trying* to relax. 'Trying' and 'relax' are complete opposites, as the more we push and 'try', the more relaxation escapes us. On the other hand, simply being present with no agenda, no judgement, allows relaxation to occur naturally.

Either sit in a comfortable chair with your body in a reasonably balanced yet very relaxed posture, or lie on your back on the floor or on a bed with your spine straight. If lying down, place a pillow or cushion under your head for support; you might wish to have another pillow under your knees.

It's always good to begin a meditation session with a few moments of cultivating a compassionate motivation as a basis for your practice. Set the intention that you are going to meditate for your own benefit and also for the benefit of others. By practising meditation, you are accumulating the skills through which you can eventually bring more peace into your life and also to the world around you.

Then focus your attention on your feet. Be aware of the toes of both feet simultaneously. Travel your attention up the toes into your feet, incorporating the soles, tops and heels and then move gradually up into the ankles. You're letting go of focusing on each area as you travel up to the next.

Slowly and smoothly move your focus into the calves and then travel up the legs towards your knees.

Explore the knee areas and then move up into the thighs, then to the pelvis and buttocks.

Simply feel whatever you feel or don't feel, without trying to label, judge or change anything.

Next you've arrived at the hips, then the lower abdomen and waist, after which switch your attention to your hands and fingers – focusing on both hands at the same time. Start with the fingertips and move slowly up into the hands.

Next focus on the wrists, then the forearms. Move up to the elbows, upper arms, and then the armpits and shoulders.

Throughout this process, whenever you get distracted by thoughts, memories, emotions, sounds, etc., simply return to the body area you were focusing on. The mind drifts away, and all you need to do is gently capture your attention and bring it back, using your body as the anchor.

The next step is to work with the torso, starting again at the waist and lower back, then travelling upwards, taking in all areas of the front, sides and spine, level by level.

Next you're focusing on your chest and upper back, the armpits and shoulders again, and then right up to the tops of the shoulders. Many people find there's a lot of tension in their shoulders, but it is important to remain neutral, not judging or labelling; just leave things as they are.

Then comes the neck; move up step by step and then focus on the jaw and head, moving into the mouth area – lips, teeth and tongue.

Travel up through your cheeks and nose, up into the eyes, eyebrows and then the top of your head – forehead, hairline and finally reach the crown of your head.

Focus your attention there for a few moments, just resting your awareness at that place.

Now reverse the process and travel downwards, but more swiftly, from the head down to the toes; it's a bit like a water line descending. This time simply move down in entire, larger sections, not in such a detailed way.

Once that is done, the last stage is to be present with your whole body, feeling the weight and stillness of it, either seated on the chair or lying on the floor or bed. Feel the support under you and be aware of the contact. You are fully supported by the furniture or the floor, and you don't need to hold your body up; you can completely let go.

Then start to notice the gentle movement of your breath. Breathe naturally, not trying to do anything special with the breath. Simply be present with the sensation of the body rising and falling softly with each breath. Stay with that for a few moments, and whenever you discover your mind has wandered, gently bring your focus back to feeling how the breath moves the body.

Finally, to end your session, repeat that wish of kindness, the intention to benefit yourself and others. You're reminding yourself of the compassionate basis of your meditation journey. Do this through making the mental commitment that you are meditating not only for your own benefit, but also for others.

The timing of this exercise is self-regulated, as it requires completing the entire process, which could take around 10 or 15 minutes, or longer if you wish. It's important not to rush it.

It's worth noting that some people might find the 'mindful body' practice makes them feel a little dizzy or light-headed; you may experience a feeling of being ungrounded or 'spaced out'. If that's the case, simply do the scan only from head to toes, i.e. only moving downwards, the first time slowly and the second time a little more swiftly.

Many people have complex feelings about their bodies, with issues around image, ageing, health and discomfort. A different relationship can start to emerge when we learn to use the body as a vehicle for training the mind. We move through each part of the body without applying judgement, simply *being with* the body, and thus the practice can be quite liberating.

An interesting thing about the body is that if you leave it alone and you're simply aware with less judgement, tensions begin to unravel of their own accord – like a snake that has a knot in its body. When the snake relaxes, the knot naturally opens.

GENERAL ADVICE FOR MEDITATION SESSIONS

It's important to practise meditation without thinking too much about it or judging it. The classic problem is the meditator who thinks, 'Am I meditating now? Is it happening? Am I there yet?' As soon as we think 'Am I meditating?' we are not meditating!

We tend to be programmed with a need to *feel* something, and again this becomes the meditator's enemy, waiting for a feeling to arise which we think will validate our experience. This means that we are no longer meditating, we are hunting. We grow bored very easily and seek stimulus, but in meditation it's important to simply relax into how things naturally are, without needing to feel something or to grasp at results.

Next we can work on how to make meditation into our habit, and this is very much about practising moments of mindfulness throughout the day, which is the heart of the next chapter.

CHAPTER SIX

Building the Habit

For meditation to work, it needs to become a path, a journey, rather than a random experience that we dip into from time to time. Meditation *training* means that session after session we are building positive habits, very much like going to the gym and building muscle.

Repetition creates a tendency which yields lasting effects. Our lives are run by habits; in fact, everything we do is both the result of old habits and the creation of new ones. Whenever we get upset, for example, it's because we already have that tendency within us, and at the same time we are perpetuating the habit of becoming upset again, which gradually becomes who we are (or more accurately who we *think* we are). If we can understand this point, we will see how we can change our habits and get more in charge of our lives.

Because of neuroplasticity, the repetition of training creates significant changes. The building of effective, positive habits is therefore of key importance. As we've seen, we are repeatedly connecting with our awareness during a meditation session; this strengthens good habits such as resilience, peace and happiness. The most powerful way to get this to work is to regularly sit down to meditate, and also to apply that meditation in our daily lives through practising moments of mindfulness. If repetition is needed for lasting change, it is important to try to meditate every day, and the key to progress is in how we combine that repetition with bringing mindfulness into our everyday experiences.

MINDFUL MOMENTS

Many people sit down to practise regular sessions of meditation, but forget to integrate the practice into their daily lives. That is like leaving one's meditation on the cushion and then going off to work. It won't have much effect, as 10 or 15 minutes of meditation each day balanced against many hours of distraction will hardly make a difference. We become like two people who never actually meet: the meditator and the non-meditator. What we need is both approaches: our daily session of meditation provides deep training for the mind – it's how we get to grips with dealing effectively with our thoughts; this is combined with practising small moments of mindfulness many times per day, even in busy situations, thus fully integrating the power of the meditation into our lives.

For many years I meditated for two hours every day but didn't really practise moments of mindfulness outside the sessions, and so my practice felt quite stagnant. One day while standing on a crowded underground train during rush hour in London – tired, hungry, a bit miserable and starting to feel the pressure of my schedule – I suddenly thought, 'Maybe practise what you preach?' I began to focus on the feeling of the ground under my feet, and the sway of the train. I paid attention to the strap of my bag weighing down on my shoulder, which now felt like a massage instead of pressure. I repeatedly practised small moments of this during the journey, and as a result got off the train feeling 10 years younger. Since that time, I find that tapping into that mindful state many times per day is the fast track to happiness.

Creating these regular short moments of mindful awareness – 'micro moments' – helps us not to stray too far from our meditation practice. We can keep a thread of the practice running through our day, so that it can slowly become our default state. It's like never dropping the ball, even while busy. This can radically transform our lives.

Two steps for learning how to practise 'mindful moments'

1. It is helpful to begin by choosing two or three mundane actions that you do every day: simple things such as cleaning your teeth, washing your hands, eating, walking, climbing the stairs, etc. You could use these actions as mindfulness 'triggers': while doing them, simply focus on the physicality of the task you're performing without flying off into a running commentary of thoughts. Normally when we're washing our hands, for example, we tend to be quite distracted, but here you are being fully present. The mental commentary will of course start up: 'This soap smells nice, it smells of roses. My grandmother had roses in her garden – or were they daffodils? I miss my grandmother . . .' But when you realise you've drifted away, simply bring your attention back to the hand washing, the raw experience of the here and

now. Feel the sensations, which means your mind is focused on what you are doing; feel the movement of your hands, the texture of the soap and the feeling of the water. Focusing on physical movements and sensations makes it quite easy to learn how to be mindful – you're skilfully using specific actions as 'pegs' on which to hang your mindfulness, thus building a habit. Even boring and dreaded activities, such as washing the dishes or ironing, can become quite interesting when you reframe them as opportunities for training the mind.

It is good to practise this for 30 days, which is the time it usually takes to instil a new habit. You could write down the two or three chosen actions and stick little notes around the house or on your desk, as reminders. Every morning when you wake up, remember those specific actions – it's best to use the same ones each day for a month – and commit to doing them mindfully that day. Before you go to bed at night, review the day, assessing how many times you managed to be mindful while doing those particular actions. It's important to stay curious and kind throughout this process, rather than feeling like a failure and being hard on yourself for forgetting.

2. After 30 days, the next step is to widen this out to all activities, practising micro moments of mindfulness many times per day, whenever you can remember. Now it's no longer a case of choosing specific actions as triggers, it's simply about regularly dropping into that mindful state for a few seconds each time, whatever you are doing. Again, you could use sensations, such as feeling the ground under your feet or the contact between your body and your chair, even in a noisy busy office. Or maybe you could focus on a visual object in front of you, or a sound, for a few seconds.

Tips for success

- **Don't stop** your activities in order to be mindful. You don't need to drop everything and pause in order to practise a mindful moment. That would separate mindful awareness from ordinary life: you're telling yourself that you have to *stop* in order to be mindful. Mindfulness would then have no place when you're busy and would never become fully integrated into your life. This is one of the reasons why I have emphasised bringing mindfulness to those daily actions which involve movement, such as brushing your teeth or washing your hands.

- **Don't slow down.** This means not going into slow motion, because that's also removing the mindfulness from real life. I find that people sometimes think anything 'spiritual' should involve becoming 'floaty' and trance-like, but actually the more we go down that route, the more we create a glamourised and other-worldly image of meditation, and we become more and more artificial about who we really are. A friend of mine at the monastery told me that she once decided to be really mindful for an entire day, and at some point one of the visitors came up to her and asked her if she was okay. Basically, she was going around very slowly, looking quite miserable.

  I once visited another monastery where I saw a monk cleaning a radiator, wiping it with a soft cloth in slow motion. It was painfully slow. I thought it was rather a beautiful sight, like modern dance, but not particularly useful as nobody actually lives like that.

- **Don't prolong.** This means not trying to stretch out long periods of being mindful; it can become oppressive, as if you're trying to force yourself into a mindful state and stay there, almost like making a child sit still. This will simply cause the mind to rebel and stir up tension and distraction. Small doses repeated often are far more useful. Then mindfulness becomes a place you want to be.

CONQUERING THE STRESSFUL MOMENT

When I give talks in the corporate world, I am often asked to provide a special technique which people can 'switch on' when they're stressed. I always explain that it doesn't work like that. When we're in a stressful situation, our habitual reactions take over and any thoughts of trying to be mindful will simply fly out of the window, unless we have built a *habit* of training. We cannot keep these techniques up our sleeve to be whipped out in emergencies, but if we learn to create a regular habit of meditation and the application of mindfulness in daily life, then we are developing the required strength and resilience needed as preparation for those stressful times.

I now travel quite extensively due to my teaching work. Standing in an airport queue or on a crowded train, I try to feel the ground under my feet, relax my shoulders and generate short moments of awareness. I find this incredibly nourishing and invigorating. It has completely changed my relationship with stress, and it has taught me that happiness is a skill to be developed moment by moment.

Anticipate the difficult by managing the easy.

– Lao Tzu

A step-by-step approach is best. Once you have become familiar with practising mindful moments many times per day, you will find it easier to apply that to stressful situations. Mindfulness has been established as a habit and now it's time to bring it into *all* areas of your life.

A good method is to start by working with 'easy' stress, such as whenever you're waiting for something. This can train you for those bigger moments of stress and even times of panic. When we're waiting for something, we often become tense and impatient, and we feel our time has been stolen from us. But why not take it as time *given*? Maybe you're stuck in traffic, at a red light at an intersection, standing in a queue, waiting for the kettle to boil or perhaps the Internet has crashed or slowed down. Phoning a call centre and being put on hold is great for this. There are even tiny moments, such as when you've pressed the button for the lift or you're waiting for an email to open.

During these moments we usually feel an urge to push forward, as we don't like the frustration of being stuck. Instead you could simply 'release and relax': feel the ground under your feet or the seat under your body; or maybe focus on your breathing, a sound or a visual object. Just let go into the moment.

Perhaps when you're stuck in traffic, instead of gripping the steering wheel of your car in fierce tension, you could simply relax your hold and explore the sensation of touch as you feel the texture of the wheel under your fingers. You're learning to stay calm in a situation that would normally wind you up. This can then help with the more difficult areas of your life, as calmness becomes a habitual response.

Our brains are usually wired to react with tension when we're in a difficult situation, but here we are reprogramming our systems, and learning that pressure can actually mean release. We're changing our habits and transforming how we experience things, literally building new neural pathways in the brain. It doesn't mean that we become a doormat, simply putting up with everything and not caring. It is really about keeping a cool head and not getting stressed, which is the best foundation for taking decisive action when required.

Practising mindful moments when waiting for things

also creates a different relationship with time. We would all love to have lots of holidays and time where we can just laze about doing nothing; we often complain about not having enough time off. We are, in fact, handed 'time off' on a golden plate every time we're waiting for something, if we could just learn how to appreciate those moments and use them for relaxation.

For those who work, practising these moments can bring a totally fresh meaning to the discussion around 'work–life balance'. I have always found that expression somewhat polarising as it suggests that we need to get our work under control so that we can have more of a life. If our working day is just made up of a set of reactions, and we don't possess the mental tools for transforming stress, then of course we cannot wait to get away from our work to start living our lives. The beauty of these techniques is that they help us to relax into each moment, which brings everything on to the journey of mindfulness.

Airports and train stations create interesting opportunities for training. These are gaps which we tend to fill by simply consuming: we shop, eat, spend money on things we don't really need – the captive situation leaves us with few options. We obsessively check our phone, but do we know how to *just be*? The airport could instead become a meditation retreat!

When we phone a call centre and are told we are 'number 10 in the queue', we groan and feel frustrated. If we knew how to truly relax into that gap, we might wish we were number 20 in the queue, as we have been given a great opportunity! These techniques can radically help us make friends with reality, no matter what is going on.

This new relationship with our experiences can create a sense of unconditional joy. Next time you're stuck in traffic, instead of automatically feeling grim, you might enthusiastically think, 'Oh great! Now I can do that thing I read about in that monk's book!' You're now seeing the traffic jam as a golden opportunity for training, a great chance for learning to embrace a difficult moment. This is the path to freedom as you can start to enjoy absolutely everything; you're learning how to fall in love with reality. Instead of the normal reflex of shutting down and feeling stuck, you are building pathways of joy. *That* is true happiness.

MINDFUL EATING

As a society we seem to have forgotten how to eat properly. The one-hour lunch break has more or less disappeared, and people are grabbing a sandwich and rushing back to their desks, eating while working. We eat standing up, while on our phones, scrolling through social media, racing and distracted. Eating mindfully, however, could be another way of working mindfulness into our daily habits, and it can also be very good for our health.

If we eat in a distracted manner, we won't chew our food properly – we are simply throwing it down our throats, quickly swallowing. Not chewing well means that we won't produce enough saliva, which contains the essential digestive enzymes needed to break down our food properly so that it can nourish us. The *way we eat* could be one of the factors contributing to our current obesity epidemic.

By eating mindfully, we will chew and digest the food properly. We'll be aware of what we're eating and will perhaps eat less than we think we need. One aspect of mindfulness is to have the wisdom to see what we are doing and to understand what would be most beneficial in the long term. We will notice if we are simply eating rubbish, using our body as a bin; we will see if we are eating 'emotionally', to fill a void. When I was stressed, I used to walk into those Pret cafes like a zombie and eat two cheese baguettes to calm myself down, hardly even tasting them. The mindless 'carb-loading' felt like a kind of opioid.

Mindful eating can also help us pay more attention to the ethics of our food, to consider more carefully what actually went on behind the scenes to produce the food we buy. We may also become aware that people have put a lot of effort into making the food for us, and so it's a shame that we hardly taste it.

The method for mindful eating is simply to eat with awareness. Focus on the entire process of lifting the food to your mouth, chewing and swallowing. Experience the sensations and tastes with complete attention. If you're having dinner with friends, of course it wouldn't work to sit there in silence, but you're bound to have some meals alone, and for those meals taken in company, you could simply begin by experiencing a few mouthfuls mindfully. There is always a way to integrate these practices naturally, without becoming severe.

ALWAYS PRACTISE, NO MATTER WHAT

It's quite important to get into the habit of practising daily sessions of meditation, as well as moments of mindfulness throughout the day, even when you're feeling unhappy, fatigued or unwell; that way you are learning to be with *any* present moment, not just the 'fun' ones. It's about being strong, whatever the situation. Maybe you manage to practise regular meditation until something throws you off course, such as a headache, sickness, fatigue or unhappiness. It then becomes tempting to avoid meditation; you want to put it off until you feel better, as perhaps you think your practice won't be 'good quality'. But good-quality practice is not necessarily about feeling great, it is about training in mental transformation in all situations.

During one of my long retreats I was extremely sick; I had caught typhoid before the retreat, while travelling in Asia. I was very ill, struggling to stay upright and finding it hard to function, so I asked the retreat leader to give me some time off from the schedule of meditation sessions. But he helped me to see that the practice *itself* is time off. When we're unwell, we really just want to rest, and meditation is actually a very deep form of rest. I think I had been struggling with ideas of what I thought 'good meditation' should be, and therefore the meditation had become hard work. So I propped myself up on cushions and carried on.

Meditation involves simply being with whatever is happening, trying not to judge it as good or bad. This is a great act of kindness towards ourselves, as we are learning total acceptance, freedom and thus unconditional happiness. It helps us to deal with all the various aspects of stress in our lives, as the practice has the upper hand rather than our reactivity to the stress.

Perhaps you are in physical pain, but it is possible to learn how to mindfully *be* with that – you could rest in the raw experience of the pain, which is very different from pushing it away and therefore suffering. Strictly speaking, pain is not in the body. It is a mental experience – when we feel physical pain, the mind is experiencing *resistance* to the pain. Being mindful in those painful moments means to relax into *what is,* without judging, without trying to push away the sensations. The pain won't necessarily go away, but our relationship with it changes, making it easier to handle. Learning this helps to increase our resilience and is truly the path to finding enduring happiness, as we discover how to stay positive against the odds.

* * *

KEEP IT SHORT

If as beginners we force ourselves to practise long, arduous sessions of meditation, we could end up simply creating resistance to the practice, and then we are less likely to do it every day. It's more skilful to practise short meditation sessions regularly. This is why I usually recommend beginning with 10- or 15-minute sessions; we are more likely to build a habit if it's something manageable. It's also important to try to avoid grasping at results. If we're looking for a 'quick fix' from meditation, we are likely to get frustrated and give up more easily. It is more helpful to see it as a long-term lifestyle choice and to relax into making it a natural part of who we are.

FIRST THOUGHT, LAST THOUGHT

When you wake up in the morning, does your hand immediately search around for your phone, which you then shove in front of your face before your eyes have even been able to open properly? What is your first habit of the day?

It's very helpful to make your first moment of the day,

as well as the last one before you sleep, a moment of mindfulness. Just as soon as you wake up, without even moving and getting up, simply be aware of your body, feel the weight of it lying in the bed, and feel your head against the pillow. Slowly become accustomed to the room around you. Applying this moment of mindfulness instils a powerful habit which helps it to become your default state.

Before you sleep, instead of churning the thoughts about the day, you could drift off in a mindful state; focus on the contact between your head and the pillow, and your body and the bed. Notice the gentle rise and fall of your body as you breathe naturally and without effort.

Starting and ending each day with a mindful moment helps develop the habit of keeping mindfulness close to your heart, allowing it to become more and more natural.

MEDITATION EXERCISES

1. Micro moments

Learn to practise micro moments of mindfulness in your

daily life, following the steps listed earlier in this chapter.

Step one is to choose two or three ordinary actions which you do more than once per day. Decide that you'll be mindful when you are doing them and try to build this up over 30 days. It is helpful to stick to the same actions each day, in order to instil a habit.

Step two is to practise micro moments of mindfulness many times per day, not just linked to specific actions. Use any of your senses as the focus, e.g. feel the sensations of standing, sitting or walking, look at a visual object, or listen to whatever sounds are naturally present.

When you become more used to this, you could start to deliberately apply mindfulness when you are waiting for something, thus reprogramming your stress reactions.

2. Sound
This is a meditation practice that uses sound as the focus for the mind.

First get into a good posture. Sit on a firm chair, with your spine straight, not leaning against the back of the chair. Place a cushion behind the base of your spine, if you wish. Your feet are flat on the floor, in parallel. Your body is balanced.

Your hands are resting in your lap, with the palms facing upwards, right on top of left, the ends of the thumbs touching; or you can place your hands with the palms down on your knees or thighs.

Lengthen the back of your neck ever so slightly by tucking in your chin a little. Place the tip of your tongue lightly against the roof of your mouth, just touching the area behind the top row of teeth. Your lips and teeth are not clenched shut, but not hanging open; there is just a little bit of space between them. Breathe through your nose if you can, otherwise breathe through your mouth.

Your eyes are open – soften your gaze and look slightly downwards, but without leaning your head forward. You're looking into the space in front of you, not at anything in particular. Blink whenever you need to.

Begin by setting an intention of kindness. Remind yourself that your practice will gradually help you to find true freedom and happiness, and then you'll be more able to bring those qualities into the lives of others. This is the motivation of compassion.

Spend a few moments feeling the ground under your feet, then shift your focus to the areas where your body is in contact with the chair. Next, be aware of your shoulders.

That was all preparation for the session. The main meditation is to use sound as the focus. Turn your attention to the sounds that you naturally hear. There will always be something, even a subtle background noise.

Our ears are always open, always hearing, but we only register the sounds when our awareness is focused through the ears. In a previous chapter I used the example of a monkey living inside a house with five windows representing the sense 'doorways'. With this practice, we are getting the 'monkey-mind' to settle at one window – in this case the sense of hearing.

When doing this meditation, it is important to try not to label or judge the sounds, drifting off into a running commentary; just hear whatever you hear without thinking about it too much.

Maybe there is a mixture of constant and sudden sounds. For example, you might be listening to the ongoing noise of a river or traffic, and occasionally a dog barks. Try to see all the sounds as the same. There is no need to separate them out and label them – just listen to that wall of sound in a neutral manner, as if for the first time ever with nothing to compare it to.

The main point is that you are being completely present, and sound is the anchor which keeps you in the moment. Whenever you realise that your mind has wandered, bring your attention back to the sounds – it means that your awareness has drifted away from your ears, and now you can bring it back.

To end the session – it is good to time it at 10 or 15 minutes – focus on your body for a few moments: feel the chair under you, and then be aware of the ground under your feet.

The last step is to again remind yourself of the intention of kindness. Think about how your practice is an offering of compassion to yourself and others.

This practice can, of course, be done in a noisy place. Usually when we meditate and there is a lot of noise, we feel it has ruined our session, but here you are incorporating that noise, in fact *using* it as the meditation. In this way, you are making friends with distraction.

The practice can also, however, be done in a relatively quiet place. There will always be some sound, even if it's just the internal noise of blood rushing in your head or a ringing in your ears.

CHAPTER SEVEN
Going Deeper

Once I had taken lifelong monk's vows, my teacher Akong Rinpoche took me under his wing; I worked with him in his office and accompanied him as his assistant when he travelled on teaching tours. The experience of spending intense amounts of time on the road, close to somebody who had such an incredible mind, and who was a living example of compassion, remains the most inspiring and enriching experience of my life. We worked closely together for almost 20 years, until Rinpoche tragically passed away in 2013. I miss him every day, but I remain filled with all that he taught me, and I feel inspired to carry on doing the work he showed me how to do.

Under Rinpoche's guidance, I began to teach meditation in Buddhist centres, but I also felt strongly drawn to engage in social work, and so I gradually began to provide meditation classes in hospitals, schools, refugee charities and drug-rehabilitation centres. Encouraged by Rinpoche, I also started to work within the corporate sector. This was before the days when mindfulness became popular, so I was a bit of a 'lone wolf'. I did, however, find people incredibly responsive, and my work took me into a wide variety of places, including prisons where I tried to help the inmates with their anger issues and stress levels.

The first time I taught in a prison was quite a tense experience for me. I was taken into various cells to do one-to-one work with those prisoners who were too vulnerable to mix with the others. One man had hands caked with dried blood and I was told he was self-harming. Another was a serial rapist who had denied his crimes; the walls of his cell were completely covered with magazine pictures of naked women, with no spaces between the photos. I spent an entire day in the sex offenders' wing, where they had their own inmates' kitchen, and I remember being struck by the fact that a group of five paedophiles had cooked my breakfast.

I got the feeling I was inside a large metal container with a group of men who felt very bad about life, the world and themselves. They were literally rattling the bars of their cage and shouting as I walked between buildings, closely guarded. These were troubled men, some with a lot of anger, and it seemed to me they'd simply been locked away without much help for their minds.

I was there to provide meditation advice, and initially I felt quite out of my depth. But things began to click when I was put in front of a group of prisoners and was asked to provide a longer, more immersive class for them. At first they were quite aggressive with me, but when I started talking about unhappiness, stress and anger from a very human perspective, without any hint of preaching, they began to melt.

I had noticed that the overwhelming sound in the prison was the noise of clashing metal as the automatic doors repeatedly opened and closed, so I talked to the prisoners about using those sounds as their meditation focus. I explained that they could turn the noise of the doors into a *method* for bringing their minds back to the present moment as they meditated, and how the very sound which was normally a constant reminder of their incarceration could become a mindfulness 'trigger', bringing them to a state of peace and calm. I also mentioned that some people pay significant amounts of money to do meditation retreats – to go to places that are completely cut off from the world, but that here they had this for free. They found this hilarious, but when I told them that I myself was planning to go into a four-year retreat, they were visibly struck. I suggested that actually they could use their time in prison for deep mental transformation.

This chapter explores some of the deeper benefits of meditation. Perhaps our initial aim in deciding to meditate may have been to feel happier and less stressed, but as we progress we can experience far greater outcomes as our minds begin to transform.

To understand this, we first need to revisit the question of what we think happiness *is*.

THE WELL-BEING TRAP

These days a key motivator for many people drawn to meditation and mindfulness is a wish to enhance feelings of well-being. We often hear the term 'inner happiness', but in fact that *search* for happiness is a tricky business. The very attempt to seek happiness can become endless, and trying to get rid of our stress can just create more of it. Meditation itself then becomes a new kind of hamster wheel on which we run without getting anywhere.

As we've seen, through *searching* for happiness from the world around us, we are identifying with a lack of happiness – 'I need it because I don't have it.' The more we grasp and cling, the more disappointment we are going to experience. The same issue arises with 'inner' happiness. If we are meditating *for* well-being, we are telling ourselves we *don't have* that well-being; and so we perpetuate a state of deficiency. Additionally, the more we try to get rid of our stress, the more we are focusing on *having* that burden of stress, and the very act of pushing it away creates more of it to push away. Habits lead to more habits.

Many people experience this and end up saying, 'Oh I tried meditation, but it didn't make me feel good, so I tried something else.' This reflects the cultural disease of our times – the quest for the 'feel-good factor', and the endless shopping around. We start shopping around in our meditation practice; hunting for a good feeling.

I went to the monastery to feel better. I was incredibly unhappy and physically very unwell. I started to meditate in quite an addictive manner. My first job as a monk was to make the beds in the monastery's guest house; it was the 'dream job', as you could take as long as you liked over it and I am quite a lazy person. I would often sit down to meditate in the rooms I was cleaning. Sometimes

I would also practise seated on little rocks in the garden; I would be walking around and then would just plonk myself down to meditate. I thought I was being really hardcore, meditating like an expert, but after a few weeks I was shocked to find I was feeling quite depressed, with a heavy, sinking feeling in my heart.

I spoke to my teacher and told him that meditation was making me depressed. He looked me squarely in the eyes and said, 'You're a junkie.' I was quite surprised, but he then explained to me that I was meditating like someone taking drugs, looking for a high; the more I was trying to feel something, the more my grasping and expectation were leading to feelings of disappointment. This conversation was a turning point and it helped me to become less fixated on results.

In Chapter One we explored how modern life is dominated by the search for the quick fix, the 'high'. People become obsessed with having their senses stimulated and happiness gets boiled down to a 'buzz' or a sensation. When we start learning meditation, it is easy to bring that same mentality with us: wanting to get a 'hit' from our practice – almost like drinking lots of caffeine or taking drugs, we want to get some sort of feeling from it. We often think we need to 'feel' something in order to know that it's working, especially these days where sensory stimulation is so high on the agenda in our culture. This becomes enormously frustrating when we sit down to meditate.

We wait for a special experience or feeling to happen, but can end up feeling worse. When we are grasping after a good experience, we're not going to get it. As already described, grasping creates more grasping: we're perpetuating that habit, simply creating more of it, and it becomes endless. Whatever happens isn't actually satisfying because the grasping has already jumped over it, looking for the next thing – our grasping mind is racing ahead thinking, 'Oh when am I going to arrive?' This is of course how many of us live our lives, walking around wondering what the 'next thing' is, and now we start doing that with the meditation.

This is the eternal hunger that drives our lives, and when we bring that into our meditation practice, we simply end up disappointed. Just as in my story, we can begin to feel quite depressed, with an experience of low energy, our heart sinking in sadness. We then start to blame the meditation, almost like someone blaming their romantic partner for not making them happy. We start questioning why, when we've done so much meditation, we are feeling miserable. We end up believing that meditation is harmful and that we should give it up and try something else.

Of course, it can't be the meditation that made us sad. If we truly analyse it, meditation isn't actually *anything* – we're just sitting there doing nothing. The problem is that due to our grasping, we demean and belittle our experience of the present moment – it doesn't feel good enough. We're not happy because our approach to happiness is all about chasing something, that proverbial pot of gold at the end of a rainbow, and getting there as quickly as possible.

A question which often comes up when I am teaching in corporate environments is, 'So how long do I have to do this before I'm better? If I do this for a month, is it done?' Corporates would like to draw a graph or make a spreadsheet of profit and loss regarding their meditation training. We always have a good laugh about this together. It's as ridiculous as somebody asking, 'What if I go running for a month? Will I be fit, and then can I stay in bed eating crisps for the rest of my life?'

The question here is – what is that *thing* people are aiming for? What is the 'endgame'? Is there a final 'hit' that will be enough for us? Some people in California are taking small recreational doses of DMT (dimethyl-tryptamine), which is thought to be the chemical released by the body at the point of death. People looking for the latest high are ingesting the 'death chemical', but they still have to go to work the next morning. It's a very interesting question: 'and then what?'

Chasing the 'high' has spiralled out of control in our culture. If our meditation practice becomes part of that race, it can only lead to problems, as previously explained. Feeling good can, of course, be a by-product of the practice, but if that's the ultimate aim, we are missing the point. This is the crux of the happiness question. Happiness will come when we stop searching for it, and we instead learn to relax into the present moment, letting go of expectation and fear. Let's ask ourselves again what we think happiness *is*: is it a sugar-rush high, or stable contentment and freedom?

CREATIVITY

One of meditation's deeper benefits is the unlocking of creativity. Even those of us who are not artistic would like to be more creative, in terms of how we live our lives and also in how we solve problems.

The factor which usually impedes our creativity is stress; we get wrapped up in a small way of thinking, where there's little room for insight or for good ideas to flow. Meditation can lower our stress and put us into a place where we're able to approach life in a more multifaceted, creative way. If we can 'get out of our own way', it can clear the space for us to have innovative ideas. As greater spontaneity arises, we can employ more originality in our thinking and in how we solve problems.

Many people who work in office environments tell me that a lot of their time is spent 'putting out fires' – ploughing through the endless administrative tasks on their plates, with too little time left for 'bigger-picture' thinking. A Stanford study published in 2009 suggested that living with so many inputs from multiple types of information simply lowers our IQ – essentially, we become more stupid when we are fragmented in our thinking and in our work. Multitasking is becoming an outdated mode of being, as it has been shown to slow the brain and kill productivity. It is far more effective to move into what I call 'fully tasking'. This means to be present and to do one thing at a time, with mindful precision. Through this we can get lots more done. Fully tasking could involve setting aside an hour for putting out those administrative fires, and then spending an hour engaging in 'bigger-picture' thinking. It also means using a mindful approach to doing things wholeheartedly and with joy.

To step into this deeper creativity, we need to discover how to live more in the present.

The present

When teaching in Iceland I visited one of the world's most beautiful places, a geyser where boiling water shoots out of the ground every 10 or 15 minutes. Hundreds of people were gathered around the crater, holding smartphones in the air waiting to photograph the eruption, probably ready to post it all online. We seem to have lost touch with the present moment – we are obsessed with capturing it for later; and so there is always a 'later' to think about.

The Internet age has of course brought us many benefits, but it has made us more absent. Our bodies may be here in the room, but our minds tend to be somewhere completely different. Our phones and the general pace of life can make us feel mentally all over the place, as if we are inhabiting several moments all at the same time. In the past people would lose themselves in a novel, but today we are facing fast-moving, multiple levels of distraction, which are far more unsettling.

People spend large amounts of money to be in the present moment, but the beaches and swimming pools of holiday resorts are full of people checking their phones. Unless we have trained our minds, we simply don't know how to be present. When we near the end of our lives we might well ask ourselves how much we were actually there for. We spent so much time living for the 'next thing', that the next thing never actually arrived – because our habit has always been to jump ahead to the 'next-next' thing.

At this point we might wonder – if we were to live more in the present, how would we ever plan for the future? Actually, the future will occur in the best way possible if we are fully mindful in the present, as right now we are sowing the seeds for a successful future; and when we do need to think about the future, if we can learn to keep our minds present while doing the planning, not thinking about something different, it will give those plans more precision, thus leading to better outcomes.

Through practising regular sessions of meditation and learning to bring mindfulness into daily life, we are repeatedly connecting with the present moment. Once we become more familiar with how to be present, we'll have more space to be creative, as our minds become less distracted. Then we can begin to play with life in interesting ways.

I give a large number of public talks, and I hardly ever prepare. I don't sit backstage revising from notes or planning what to say. I find that by fully embodying the present moment the right words will come, and with impact. When somebody in the audience asks me a tricky question, my old habit would have been to get nervous and to tense up, but I find that if I relax completely, I can give a helpful answer. I've discovered that learning to meet pressure with space is the key to creativity.

MENTAL FOCUS

Our powers of concentration, or mental focus, can become significantly enhanced if we meditate regularly.

Many people think of meditation simply as a relaxation technique, which they see as a kind of switching off or drifting away, and so there is a concern that it would *reduce* focus. In fact, the opposite is true.

As I mentioned, I started to teach meditation in the corporate world many years before the current rush of interest in mindfulness, so there wasn't really a common language for it. It felt like working from the ground up, where I had to break through a lot of misconceptions. I once went into a small company in London to teach meditation to the staff. Their boss had read about me in the news and had invited me in, but he seemed reticent. Before I was allowed into the boardroom, he took me into a small room – it felt like a job interview – and said,

'Look, I'm really impressed with what you do, it's great. I'm so happy you're here, but please don't make them too relaxed.' I asked him what he meant, and he said he didn't want his staff to become useless.

I found this exchange fascinating. It suggested he thought I was somehow going to hypnotise his staff and put them into a trance, or that they'd become so relaxed from the meditation that they would end up lounging around not answering the phones or doing any work. He thought they would be like zombies with no drive or efficiency. The perceived image of relaxation is that it's quite a passive state, where we lose our 'edge'. I explained to him about meditation and mental focus, and we had a great session.

In a 'disaster movie', where people are trapped in a burning elevator or the end of the world is coming, there's usually that one person who stays calm and saves the day. They're an example of strong focus with a sense of calm. They are not rushing around like a spinning top, but neither is their state of relaxation floppy or dopey; they are highly efficient. Mindful, relaxed focus means we don't lose our edge; if anything, that edge becomes sharper and more accessible.

At the end of this chapter you'll find a meditation exercise which uses your breathing as the support. This greatly enhances mental focus as you'll be learning to pay attention in a concentrated, yet relaxed manner, bringing your awareness to very precise sensations.

DECODING OUR ADDICTIONS

As our meditation training progresses, we'll be drilling down deeper in terms of mental transformation. One aspect of that is to understand and change our addictive habits.

An addiction is where we feed a habit, often without even wanting to, and it becomes detrimental to our happiness. The roots of this lie in our deepest addiction, which is to our thoughts and emotions – they arise, and we jump in and cling on to them, even when we don't want to. Based on this internal addiction, we can become addicted to all kinds of outer things.

Addiction is rather like scratching an itch for relief, where the more we scratch, the worse the itch becomes. Instead, through being mindful we can discover some space between impulse and action. In that space we can begin to make choices – maybe not to scratch.

When we are addicted to something in the world around us, we are reaching for that thing to alleviate the discomfort of wanting: to 'get rid' of the feeling. The activity to which we are addicted eventually no longer feels pleasant as much as just being a form of relief. This is symbolic of life as a whole: we spend our energy seeking relief, constantly trying to extinguish the flames of wanting, but the wanting never ends. A solution to this can be to 'turn around' and look at the wanting mind itself, rather than focusing on the object of the wanting. When we stare wanting directly in the face, something interesting happens: it begins to dismantle, as if it is unable to withstand the glare of awareness. We can do this by using the craving feeling itself as the 'object' of meditation, focusing on its sensation without judging it; this is like looking directly at the craving rather than following its dictates.

Addiction means we are feeling a kind of lack, or an emptiness, within ourselves, and we are trying to 'fill that hole'. Addicts often speak of the 'hole in the soul'. Of course, through chasing and getting an object of our desire, we are simply deepening that hole, as we perpetuate the feeling of needing something in order to feel fulfilled. Meditation can fill us up from within. It is called 'mindfulness', but one could easily use the term 'mind-full-ness'. It is not about emptying the mind, but instead filling the mind with peace, joy and fulfilment.

When we rest mindfully in the present moment, we can discover that everything we ever wanted is right here. That's because whenever we want something, we are seeking a feeling of completion, a feeling of *having* what we want. It is not the thing itself that we want, what we are looking for is that *feeling*. When we are in a mindful state, we are resting in that completeness; we are relaxing into the moment without wanting it to be different.

UNDER THE FLOORBOARDS

'What in me is dark, Illumine'.

– John Milton, *Paradise Lost*

As we go deeper in our practice, we might wonder what's going to 'come up'. We may feel afraid that we're going to have to face our past, or meet our own darkness in some way. Will our 'unconscious material' begin to surface during the practice?

For the path of meditation, it is most helpful to view the mind in terms of what I would call 'context rather than content'. Perhaps we assume we ought to explore the 'content': '*Why* do I feel the way I feel? What happened in my past? Where did all this come from?' We might even worry that if we don't dig everything up from 'under the floorboards', we will never be free.

Meditation practice, however, focuses on the mind itself, i.e. the 'context', and transforms the habitual manner in which that mind *relates* to its content – how it grabs and holds on to it. The meditation journey is thus about seeing *how* rather than *why* we are suffering.

When we meditate using our breathing as a focus (see the exercise at the end of this chapter), we are learning to repeatedly return our focus to the breath when we realise our attention has wandered. Perhaps we were simply thinking about what to eat for lunch or other mundane thoughts, but every time we return to the breath, we are thinning down that mental 'glue' which solidifies and holds on to the mind's content. Training repeatedly in this way will therefore disempower the hold our psychological 'unconscious material' seems to have on us. That material will naturally start to have less power and can start to dissolve, as the attachment in the mind reduces and we begin to discover a pure awareness that lies beyond the suffering like the sky behind the clouds.

Could working like this carry a risk of denial or suppression? The interesting thing is, we cannot repress something that isn't actually real. Meditation practice introduces us to the illusory nature of our problems, and shows us that our thoughts and feelings are without solidity. If, on the other hand, we are locked into seeing the material from our past as solid and real, then it is bound to feel as if we are pushing something down, and this will create an internal pressure that can make us suffer.

The solution, then, is to take a position of awareness, where we can discover a bigger mind than the suffering with which we've identified so strongly up to now in our lives. Perhaps, therefore, it is not that we need to 'sort out' our psychological material from the past, but instead we can resolve the past by changing how our minds function in the present. Maybe we don't need to reorganise the content, or to keep searching for answers inside it. That searching can feel like digging around looking for a golden key, but the very act of digging becomes endless, creating more material as we dig.

When we feel as if we are trapped in a house with many rooms with locked doors, and each room contains a lot of mess, we might think we have to find different keys for each of those doors, and that we need to go in and clean up the mess in each room, one by one. Through meditation, however, we are creating *one key* that can open every door – we have found a 'master key' – as meditation helps us realise that our thoughts and emotions are not solid in the first place; actually, there is no mess to clean up.

We can find this master key simply through breathing.

MEDITATION EXERCISES

1. Breathing meditation

At this point we're going to start working with our breath, which is probably the most well-known traditional meditation practice. In Chapter Five, we began our practice by using our body as the main focus, and now we'll be going deeper.

Below is a seven-step method for meditation on the breath – if the session has a clear structure, it's easier to stay focused, as there are tangible steps to follow. Step five is the one to spend longest on, with the others taking just a few moments each. For beginners, it's good to time a 10- or 15-minute session in total.

1 Settle into a good posture. Sit up straight on a firm chair; you can place a small cushion behind the base of your spine. Your back is straight, not leaning against the back of the chair, unless you have physical difficulties. Your feet are in parallel, flat on the floor. Your body is balanced and upright, yet relaxed.

• Your hands are resting in your lap, with the right hand on top of the left, palms facing upwards with the tips of the thumbs touching. Or you can place your hands with the palms down on your knees or thighs.

• Lengthen the back of your neck ever so slightly, by tucking in your chin a little. Place the tip of your tongue lightly against the roof of your mouth, just touching the area behind the top row of teeth.

• Your lips and teeth are neither clenched shut nor hanging open; there is just a little bit of space between them. Breathe through your nose if you can, otherwise, of course, breathe through your mouth.

• Your eyes are open. Soften your gaze and look down-wards slightly but without letting your head lean forward. You're not looking around the room, but just into the space in front of you, and not at anything in particular. Blink whenever you need to.

2 Set an intention of kindness. Spend a few moments reminding yourself that your practice will help you to find greater peace and happiness, and the ability to bring those qualities to others. This is the motivation of compassion: the commitment to help yourself and others.

3 Take a few moments to feel the ground under your feet. Shift your focus to the areas where your body is in contact with the chair. Then feel the texture of the clothing under your hands, without moving your fingers about. Next be aware of your shoulders and then bring your attention down to your abdomen.

4 Start to notice how your breath repeatedly and subtly moves your body with a gentle contraction and expansion. You might feel this in your abdomen or higher up. Breathe naturally, without effort, not trying to breathe deeply or in any particular way.

• Your mind will keep wandering away throughout this process, and that's completely fine – remember this is your opportunity to bring back your focus, at this stage to the body, again and again.

5 This is the step to spend the longest time on. Bring your attention to your face and feel where the air is coming in and out, again breathing naturally with no force. If you can breathe through your nose, feel the air coming in and out of the end of your nose; notice the subtle movement of air at the edge of the nostrils. If you need to breathe through your mouth, focus on how the air feels against your lower lip.

• This step engages quite a precise focus, which really aids the meditation, as you are generating the ability to concentrate as well as repeatedly coming back to the focal point when your mind wanders. Every time you return to the breath, you are building the ability to get less entangled in your thoughts and emotions.

6 When you're ready to end the session, focus on your body for a few moments – feel the chair under you, and then be aware of the contact with the ground under your feet.

7 The last stage is to remind yourself of the intention of kindness. Think that your practice is an offering of compassion to yourself and others.

2. Counting the breaths

For this exercise use all the above steps, but replace step five with the following:

Mentally count your breaths, with the complete cycle of the in-breath and out-breath being one number. Again, remember to breathe naturally and without effort. These are not deep breathing exercises. Try to count up to seven cycles, and then return to number one and start again. Whenever you lose count, it means your mind has wandered, so simply restart from number one.

When you become stronger at doing this without losing focus, extend the goal to 21 cycles. I have met people who can count 1000 cycles (I definitely can't!).

CHAPTER EIGHT

Happiness is a Group Effort

Up to this point we have been looking at meditation from an individual perspective; the next step is to widen the focus and explore how it can enhance our relationship with the world around us.

We are all intricately linked to others; in fact, we are connected to everything – we are *interconnected*. In Buddhism this is described through the term 'inter-dependence': everything depends on everything else for its existence.

We can see this by considering the most fundamental, basic thing we do – breathing. Breathing keeps us alive, yet we cannot breathe alone – our ability to breathe depends, in an interconnected way, on the world around us. The trees and plants use sunlight and carbon dioxide to produce the oxygen that we breathe; as we exhale, we in turn contribute to the carbon dioxide they need to produce more oxygen. This interdependent relationship with our surrounding world is a metaphor for everything in our lives.

Our survival, as well as our happiness, relies on others. The food we eat and the clothes we wear – in fact our very existence – depend upon others. If we don't respect this fact, we cannot find true happiness.

THE CELEBRATION OF THE SELF

Historically we had more of a 'pack' or tribe mentality. Community was held in high esteem, and we lived with a sense of the larger group, both socially and in family life, which engendered a feeling of cohesion. Our culture has now, however, moved into a phase where the individual is seen as more important than the community – we celebrate self-empowerment. A lot of the inputs we receive through advertising, social media and even music tell us 'it's all about you'. The focus now is on self-identity, and this seems to have made us rather lonely.

Many children and teenagers grow up today with wild ambitions, where the plan is simply to become rich and famous; celebrities are seen as gods. A typical childhood wish is to become a pop star, a footballer or a Kardashian. It's perfectly natural to be drawn to something that feels empowering, but perhaps we tend to look in places which are ultimately unsatisfying. The more wrapped up in the 'self' we become, the further we stray from genuine happiness. The self is run by desire and aversion, and as we've seen, those habits simply create more of themselves, where nothing is ever good enough or feels safe enough, and this makes it impossible to achieve sustainable happiness.

That aim for the total realisation of the self has also permeated the worlds of 'self-help' and mindfulness, with a desire to become the 'best you', to achieve complete 'self-actualisation', and so on. Through this we can easily fall into the trap of perpetually grasping after an illusory sense of well-being, leading to the frustrations which I described in Chapter Seven (see p. 114).

Who is this 'self' anyway? If we were to investigate, we might find there is no separate, independent, autonomous entity that we can actually call the self. If we explore who we are, what *is* our identity? Are we our bodies? Our bodies come from others, from the cells of our parents, the nutrients in the womb, from all the food that we eat; and what we eat comes from others too. What then in the body is the part that we truly own?

Classic Buddhist meditations pose the question, is the self really in the body? If so, *where* in that body are 'we' located? If we were to lose an arm, of course there'd be a physical difference, but would the 'self' reduce or diminish by a corresponding amount?

Is the self in the mind? If we examine our consciousness, we simply find a stream of instants, none of which can be pinned down as 'us'. The past moment is dead, the future is yet to come, and where is the present? As soon as we pin it down, it has gone, it is already a past moment.

Even the 'observer' – the part of the mind that seems to be aware when we meditate – is not a 'self'. Just as we can see but cannot touch the sky, we can experience observing but cannot identify an observer. The 'self' is simply, then, a concept. We only exist in relation to others, and until we honour that we will always feel as if something is missing.

In modern times we all want to be unique and special. Our uniqueness, however, is really a product of everyone and everything we have come into contact with. We are very interested in defining who we are, but this individual can only be defined in relation to others.

Extreme examples of this are leaders and people who are famous. They depend on having an audience. Those who have power over others *need* those others. The famous require other people to make and keep them famous; they are in many ways enslaved to their public. It is an interdependent relationship.

GRATITUDE FOR OUR CONNECTIONS

Our happiness, survival and very existence thus depend on others, and others depend on us, no matter who we are. If we can tap into, acknowledge and understand this interconnection, then a positive feeling can arise towards the world at large, and that feeling is *gratitude*.

Our culture does not particularly promote gratitude. We are conditioned to look at what's missing in our lives, so that we will feel compelled to try to obtain more, rather than being content with and grateful for what we have. We are encouraged to compete and win, through which our relationships can become quite transactional, constantly assessing what others can do for us. By not recognising how much others have contributed to our very existence, we easily fall into the traps of selfishness and unkindness. If, on the other hand, we begin to feel grateful, it can make us feel closer to everyone else, and that will create a sense of responsibility, just as in a family unit.

To find genuine, enduring happiness, it is helpful to feel gratitude and to honour the interconnection between all beings, otherwise we just become entrenched in a selfish mindset, which gives rise to more desire and more aversion. An openness to our connectivity, and the compassion which can arise through that, are much more aligned with our natural state.

We all have a natural capacity to feel connected. We see this in children and how they respond to others. If a child sees another child laughing or crying, they will often join in. Children are very open: they will walk up to others with very few barriers, they are less self-conscious than adults and they have a natural impulse to connect. This tendency diminishes as we grow, but even as adults we are naturally inclined to find great joy in a sense of community. We like to laugh in groups, and if I yawn, you will yawn too.

When I came out of my four-year retreat, I arrived in London feeling very present and open-hearted. I had a strong impulse to go up to people on the street and hug them, and I quickly had to rein this in! It is not socially acceptable. Yet deep in our being we *do* have a wish to connect. When we see others in pain, a mirroring effect occurs within our brains – our corresponding pain centres are activated, which indicates that our brains are wired for empathy. We also have a neurological basis for kindness: when we do something kind, there is an activation in the brain's reward system, the nucleus accumbens, which then produces chemicals which make us feel good. Without this hard-wired kindness we would not actually have survived as a species; we are programmed to reach out and help each other.

Stress, however, is one of the most powerful suppressants of our natural kindness and connectivity. When we are stressed our minds tend to 'shrink' and we have no space to think of others. We have so much in common – we all want to be happy and free from suffering – yet our busy lives can make us feel separate from each other.

UNNATURAL RESOURCES

Many aspects of modern life separate us from feeling connected. The resources we draw upon for our happiness feel artificial and unsatisfying when the focus is on externals, such as how we look and what we have. Living in an era of competition and comparison inhibits our natural sense of connection and engenders isolation. Life so often becomes a battle to be won; the phrase 'to get ahead' implies having to race against others. Consumer culture requires us to think as an individual rather than for the whole, as it's that separation which keeps the wheels turning. We 'look out for Number One', but at what cost?

Nowadays our experience of connection is often reduced to the 'worldwide web', usually via social media. But the more 'connected' we've become through the Internet, the more isolated we have grown from those around us. Through this type of interaction, our connections can remain quite shallow, where we amass 'friends' like numbers. We scroll through those connections, automatically clicking 'like' on photos and then scrolling on, but this almost mindless act doesn't give us a sense of being in a real relationship or feel like true sharing. Sometimes we go through our social media 'feeds' and we tap 'like' on everything as a type of duty, as if doing our homework. Instagram even tells us 'You're all caught up.'

We often feel more interested in what's happening on the other side of the world than in what's right in front of us. Perhaps that feels safer as it requires less from us emotionally. We can find it hard to be fully present in our relationships. In some families, individuals take their meals at different times so that they don't have to encounter each other, or they sit hunched over, lost in their phone screens while at the dining table.

I recently had dinner with an old friend, during which he seemed to manage to hold a sort of conversation with me while sending WhatsApp messages to a few different girls with whom he was flirting. He described it as 'keeping the plates spinning'. These days distraction has become highly addictive. When we are out for dinner or for a coffee, how often do we keep our phones on the table, fingers twitching to check what might be going on?

NATURAL RESOURCES

Our lack of understanding regarding interdependence has led us to severely harm the environment. We have a limitless desire for comfort, and our greed and levels of consumption have caused a serious crisis on our planet. Our desire goes completely unchecked, and is in fact encouraged. We don't behave in a way which reflects how connected everything is, and thus we are reckless.

Our problem lies in thinking that happiness comes from material objects. These objects aren't inexhaustible, whereas our desire is. Perhaps we have a habit of taking long, luxurious showers while many people across the world have nothing to drink, or no access to clean, safe water. Being more mindful of this could help to save lives. All that is needed is to be more aware and careful with our resources. Who owns the world's resources anyway? Surely we all do, equally. If we can wake up to interdependence, it will help us want to share.

Sustainable living requires us to change the mindset concerning *where* we think happiness actually comes from. Simply recycling our waste, while important, is not enough. What needs to change is our level of greed; this will only happen when we understand that greed does not lead to happiness. We urgently need to realise that happiness comes from within, which is something boundless and limitlessly recyclable.

Meditation in the 21st century is very much about saving our planet through changing our minds. If we don't work on this, then even if we *do* think that happiness comes from the things around us, quite soon there won't be anything left to 'make' us happy anyway. We are now in crisis and we need to wake up.

THE POWER OF CONTENTMENT

If we change our inner attitude and learn to feel content, then and only then can the earth support us. Based on this shift in thinking, we can act mindfully, and we should feel confident that what we do *will* have an effect; using mindful steps to save our resources will definitely be of benefit. It is not wise to think, 'It's only me, so why bother?' That kind of attitude causes people not to vote in elections. But we know that every action, like every vote, counts.

We no longer have to see happiness as a competitive process. Does my happiness need to come at the cost of yours? Does your happiness take away my own? Is happiness like a cake with a finite number of slices, not enough to go around? If we think like that, happiness becomes like a war to be won.

The new zeitgeists are going to be contentment and compassion. In fact, the best foundation for a successful life is contentment, as only a content mind has the resources needed to bring about effective results. If we exist from a place of feeling lack, we will not achieve very much, as we simply carry around the feeling of 'I don't have', which then becomes our reality.

UNHEALTHY CONNECTIONS

When we don't act with wisdom, our interconnectedness can bring suffering to others. As we grow more global, it is essential that we become more aware of the effects we have on each other.

An example of this is the case of Ladakh, a state in the North of India, which is sometimes called 'Little Tibet'. It was completely closed to Western influence until around 1975, when things dramatically opened up. One of the most shocking changes was the arrival of Western advertising and tourism. The region had been totally cut off, the people there had lived in their own Shangri-La bubble, and now the West was suddenly seeping into every aspect of their lives.

This led to a number of problems, the most striking of which was that the young people began to bleach their skin. Ladakhi teenagers were looking at white faces on television and on advertising billboards – heads thrown back in laughter, sitting in fancy cars, drinking Coca-Cola, with seemingly perfect lives – and they began to resent their own beautiful brown faces. Sales of the Indian face cream 'Fair & Lovely' went through the roof.

The traditional subsistence economy had meant that all basic needs, including labour, had been provided without money. Now, with the arrival of tourists spending large sums of money, everything was thrown out of balance, and the local people began to feel poor. Crime and the notion of poverty had not really existed within their culture up until that time. What had been a society built on the principles of compassion and connection, now became one of greed and poverty, with increasing levels of drug abuse and suicide.

I think the story of Ladakh is a sad metaphor for our 21st century, where interdependence can become a type of infection rather than something supportive, because we don't connect mindfully. Furthermore, it illustrates how encouraging the mindset of comparison acts like a poison, destroying equanimity and contentment.

RELATIONSHIPS

Our first connection in life was with our mother, and this involved a chemical exchange. As soon as a baby emerges from their mother's womb, both mother and infant experience a huge spike in cortisol. This is to protect the baby from danger as they move from a water to an air environment. Ideally the baby is then placed on the mother's chest, and the skin-to-skin contact produces oxytocin in both, which is further enhanced through breast-feeding, bringing down the stressful levels of cortisol. Oxytocin is the chemical associated with feeling calm, secure and connected. Its nicknames in scientific circles are the 'cuddle chemical' and the 'moral molecule'; it makes us feel safe, and it is also the chemistry of connection.

Our mother thus introduces us to resilience, showing us that we can move from a heightened state of stress, fuelled by cortisol, to a place of safety and calm, immersed in oxytocin. She is priming us to deal with stress by instilling a state of calm, through her kindness and compassion; it is no accident that we use the phrase 'the milk of human kindness'.

This creates neural pathways of resilience in the brain, which become essential supports later in life. The baby is also being introduced to their own internal resources of the bonding chemistry of oxytocin, feeling that sense of connection.

Oxytocin arises through unconditional love, and we feel nourished when we experience it. When we understand that true happiness lies in the recognition of our connectivity to the world around us, our internal chemistry completely changes, bringing about a stable sense of calm and security.

There are other things in life that increase oxytocin – finding a close-knit community, even giving and receiving hugs. The tribe is a powerful communal unit, and it has been shown that the Maasai tribe in Africa have high levels of oxytocin. Studies have shown that oxytocin is also boosted by meditation, when practised with an altruistic component (as explained in the next chapter).

We were born to connect. Many people, however, now live crammed next to each other in houses like boxes, with thin partitions between each house, and yet perhaps they don't even know their neighbours' names. We go to sleep at night, and maybe our neighbour is also in their bed, on the other side of that wall; it's as if we are breathing in each other's faces, with only a thin wall separating us, but we don't know each other. Huge areas of our society consist of people living like that, in boxes piled up next to each other, with everybody just looking after their own needs and those of their families. Many of our social problems stem from this type of self-centred living, divorced from our natural sense of connection.

Our relationships suffer when we are selfish. There's often a type of *quid pro quo*: we want others to love us back; that's the 'deal'. Of course, that's an understandable wish, but there's a problem. In truth, we can give love, and we can receive it, but we cannot take or expect love from someone – that is impossible. The subtext of 'I love you, you love me back, here are the rules, and if the rules are broken the love will be cancelled', creates a sort of business transaction. Sometimes our very identity becomes dependent upon somebody loving us. There is often a perceived need for the other person to 'complete' us, but that means we will never feel complete, as we are simply perpetuating an illusion of incompleteness.

We struggle in relationships when there is a transmission of stress between the parties. This is a major problem in families, and when parents 'dump' their stress on their children, that stress can become internalised. The child may grow up with the inner voice of the angry parent, which becomes part of who they are, leading to self-loathing issues later in life. This acts like a lineage of suffering; our parents received it from their parents, and so on further back down the line.

Parents tend to be quite overburdened, reacting to their children's behaviour in a stressful manner. When a child is expressing emotion, a common response from a stressed parent is to simply say 'stop it' or 'no'. The child grows up with a feeling that their emotions are something to be said 'no' to, which can create an emotional disconnection within them. Emotional intelligence can be introduced to children when parents learn how not to automatically say 'no', and can instead stay mindful and open.

Engaging with meditation training is one of the kindest things you can do for yourself, for your relationships and family, and for society at large. It gives you the resilience through which you can take care of your own stress without passing it on to others. You can connect in a healthy way. You can break the chain of suffering.

MEDITATION FOR CHILDREN

When I give talks, parents in the audience often ask about meditation and mindfulness for their children. They see it as something helpful for themselves, which naturally they would like to share with their children. Parents have growing concerns regarding their kids' stress levels, where school life sometimes feels like a corporate workplace with unrealistic expectations being placed upon pupils. The Internet and particularly social media have created all sorts of issues around stress and insecurity, and parents look on in horror as their children disappear further into their phone screens. Fortunately, there is now a growing movement to bring mindfulness into schools.

I teach at several schools in the UK, where I try to implement a mindful culture to help both pupils and staff. I work with primary and secondary schools, in both the state and independent sectors. I teach meditation sessions in the classroom, and I also show teachers how they can start off a lesson with a two-minute mind-fulness exercise.

It goes without saying that children are tomorrow's leaders, and if we teach meditation to them at a young age, it can have a highly positive impact on future society.

> *If every eight-year-old in the world is taught*
> *meditation, we will eliminate violence from the*
> *world within one generation.*
>
> – His Holiness the 14th Dalai Lama

The question that parents usually ask is, 'How do I get my kids to meditate?' I think it's important not to force meditation upon anyone, especially children and teen-agers. They can easily develop a resistance towards it, viewing it as a pressure or a punishment – like being made to eat their green vegetables. There are schools in the USA where they replace detention with mindfulness sessions and I wonder if that creates an association between mindfulness and punishment. It's important to make meditation inviting and even fun, so that children form a positive association with it. It's also helpful to tailor the techniques, making them easier to understand. Shorter sessions work better.

The main advice, however, is for parents to lead by example; if you as a parent are meditating regularly, this sends a positive message to your children, positioning meditation as something normal. As your stress levels reduce, this will clearly have a beneficial effect on your children.

It is also helpful in family life to use a lot of language connected to compassion and kindness; this can instil in children a sense of how important those qualities are. This again needs to be done in a way which doesn't feel like a harsh duty. My grandmother used to order me to be kind, and she would force me to write thank you letters. There was an implication that I was bad for not having thought of it myself, and so I used to feel quite resentful about the whole matter!

In summary, we are creatures of connection. Deep down, kindness is our true nature, and genuine happiness is only possible when we acknowledge our connectivity. This recognition leads to compassion, which is the subject of the next chapter and is the key to finding a happiness that endures and which respects how connected we all are.

MEDITATION EXERCISES

1. Focusing on natural objects

This first exercise uses objects around us as meditation supports, building a mindful connection with the outside world.

You're going to place a small object on a table in front of you and focus your eyes on it. This may sound simple, but you'll find your attention will constantly wander away, and the skill is in training to return to the object.

You'll be using an object from nature – a pebble, a short stick or the flame of a candle. You're connecting with the natural things of the world around you, engaging with them in a mindful way.

Choose just one of those objects. If it's a pebble or a short stick, try to find one that is quite smooth and relatively uniform in colour. If you're using a candle, a simple one will do. Place the chosen object in front of you, not too close and not too far away, at about the level of your chest. The ideal background is blue, but at least find a table or tablecloth without patterns, as that will be too distracting.

Sit with a good posture, upright on a chair. You can place a small cushion behind the base of your spine. Your back is straight, not leaning against the back of the chair. Your feet are in parallel, flat on the floor. Your body is balanced. Your hands are resting in your lap, or with the palms down on your knees or thighs. Your chin is slightly tucked in and the tip of your tongue is touching the roof of your mouth, just behind your teeth. Your eyes are open, and you'll be looking at the object in front of you for most of the session.

Begin the session by setting an intention of kindness. Remind yourself that your practice will help you to find genuine happiness which you can then share with others, as we are all interconnected. This is the motivation of compassion.

Then spend a few moments feeling the ground under your feet. Next shift your focus to where your body is in contact with the chair. Finally, be aware of your shoulders.

The major part of the session is then spent looking at the object in front of you – the pebble, stick or candle flame. If you're using a candle, look at the middle of the flame.

Keep your gaze focused on the object, remembering to blink whenever you need to, and when your mind wanders bring your attention back to where your eyes are looking.

Sometimes your eyes might feel sore. If that happens, just close them for a few seconds.

You're not *thinking about* the object; you're simply being aware of it without distraction. When you do get distracted, gently bring your attention back. You're not staring blankly; your awareness and sense of focus are fully engaged.

Sometimes there might be visual distortions, where it can seem as if the object is moving or changing shape. This is just an optical illusion caused by subtle tension. Again, close your eyes for a short while. It's important to stay relaxed. Maintain the focus, with your eyes and also with your mind.

To end the session, timed at 10 or 15 minutes, look away from the object and focus on your body for a few moments.

The last stage is to again remind yourself of the intention of kindness. Think about how your practice is an offering of compassion to yourself and others.

2. Gratitude practice

This practice is particularly helpful in modern times. As previously mentioned, we live in an era where now more than ever, people tend towards dissatisfaction. There is a focus on what we lack and on the negative. We are conditioned to constantly feel that there is something missing.

You can, however, teach yourself how to feel gratitude and appreciation – these can become a *training*. You can learn to truly enjoy everything. This wouldn't cause you to give up trying to achieve things – it simply means feeling fulfilled in the moment, and having a more positive mind.

Sit in a quiet place, in the usual good posture. As this is a 'thinking' practice, you can close your eyes if you wish.

Establish the best motivation for the practice, which is to generate a wish to bring greater happiness not only to yourself, but to the world at large. This is the pure intention of compassion.

Spend a few moments establishing mindfulness through feeling the weight of your body on the chair and then the ground under your feet.

Bring to mind three things in your life for which you feel grateful. They can be things, people, situations – anything. Slowly think of them one at a time, exploring why you are – or could be – grateful for them. Feel the fullest sense of appreciation and gratitude for those things.

Try to understand that everything depends on everything else. Our very survival depends on so many things around us. In this way, you can generate deep gratitude as you recollect the kindness of the world around you.

The next step is to feel happy for others. Mentally rejoice in the achievements and happiness of others. Think of people you know as well as those you don't know. Cultivate a feeling of happiness for them, a sense of delight in their success. We usually feel that way when it comes to our loved ones, but here you are extending it to strangers as well – we are all interconnected, and we can share happiness. There is enough to go around.

To end the session, after your chosen length of time – for example, 10 or 15 minutes – focus on your body for a few moments, feeling your shoulders, then the body's contact with the chair and lastly the ground under your feet.

Finally, repeat the compassionate intention with which you began the session – remind yourself that you are practising meditation for the benefit of all. As your practice begins to yield benefit, your ability to share peace and happiness with others will increase.

As with every meditation, it is helpful to practise this exercise regularly, and each time it is good to think of three new things you feel grateful for, building up a sense of gratitude and appreciation towards everything in your life.

CHAPTER NINE

Compassion

●   ●   ●

After I'd been travelling the world for almost 12 years giving talks and courses, Rinpoche said I was becoming 'a bit like a parrot', simply repeating the instructions I had heard, and he encouraged me to enter a long-term meditation retreat. The purpose was to gain a better understanding of practice, for my own development but also to be able to teach meditation from a deeper perspective, more from the heart. So in 2005 I embarked on the four-year retreat on the Isle of Arran in Scotland.

I felt quite frightened going into this retreat. Having done a nine-month retreat a few years earlier, I knew that it would be hard work and that I'd need to face the demons of my own mind; and indeed, I spent the first two years of the retreat in a state of severe depression and anxiety, regularly experiencing panic attacks and emotional turmoil. This was a shocking experience, and I found it hard to fully engage with the practices. I had a Buddha statue on a shrine in my room that I wanted to kick across the floor – the negativity in my mind was so extreme. At times I felt as if I was falling through dark space with nothing to hold on to. It was extremely humiliating, as I was one of the 'senior' monks in the retreat and yet there I was, completely falling apart.

Things reached fever pitch when I hit such a dark place that I thought I would have to leave. But from there somehow the only way was up. I had no choice but to dive into the meditations that were being taught, and then things began to change. I started to find a way to work with my pain, to *accept* it by meditating 'into' it. The second half of the four years was completely different. I discovered that happiness is like a 'switch' in the mind. I was fascinated to see how this can be accessed through compassionate acceptance of one's own pain. I began to see how we can *choose* happiness, and also the importance of compassion for oneself and others. Severe levels of self-hatred began to give way to a deeper sense of acceptance, which I feel is the foundation for being able to help others. I still have a long way to go, but I did learn something life-changing which I now try to share with others.

When I came out of the retreat I began to teach meditation again. I now always emphasise compassion at the heart of that training. I see this as the key to finding true, sustainable happiness for ourselves and, in this interdependent world, helping others to find it too.

FROM EMPATHY TO COMPASSION

We saw in the previous chapter that we are hard-wired to feel connected to others. We usually experience this as empathy, which is a feeling we encounter when we see others suffering. This can, however, be quite debilitating. Research has shown that when we see somebody suffering, brain activation occurs in the areas that correspond to what the other person is experiencing. For example, if we see someone in physical pain, the same areas in *our* brains will operate almost like a mirror. Tania Singer, a neuroscientist who has carried out extensive work in this field, describes empathy as a form of 'emotional contagion', like 'catching' the suffering of another. It's as if someone is drowning and we jump in but cannot swim, and so we drown with them; we don't know how to save them. This is not that useful, as now *two* people need help. Compassion, on the other hand, is far more dynamic, as we will see later.

Connecting with others through empathy, therefore, has limitations. It's a feeling that can lead to fatigue and stress, and as a consequence we aren't well equipped to help others. We can explore four ways in which this happens.

Emotional reactivity

Empathy is an *emotional reaction*; we see someone suffering and we are triggered. This is of course a good thing – it means that we have a heart, we are open to others – but simply *feeling* something is neither stable nor particularly useful. A feeling comes and goes; it is dependent on the right triggers and when those are absent the feeling is not present, and so the empathy is not sustainable. Also, this emotional component of empathy can simply mean that we too are now suffering, which is not really helpful to anyone.

Expectation

Empathy can lead us to be kind to others, and maybe to try to help them. This becomes tricky, however, when we want something back. Perhaps we need to feel it was 'worth it'. Often, when we've done a lot to help someone, there comes a point where we think, 'After all I've done for them . . .' We feel our work has not been recognised or repaid – we think we are owed some kind of gratitude. There is an expectation that because of what we have done for them, we should now be treated in a certain way. It can become almost like a barter system. So our empathy often contains hidden expectations.

The most painful scenario is when we do a lot to help somebody, and at some point they let us down, hurt or abuse us. Our internal voice then intensifies: 'After all I've done for them, how *could* they?' This suggests the help wasn't unconditional, there were rules under the surface. We can end up feeling that our kindness was not worth giving or has not been justified. This can be enormously frustrating.

Preference

There is usually a *preferential* quality to our empathy. We prefer particular individuals, and in the case of strangers, empathy only arises towards them when they're in certain situations. This is incredibly limiting, and where preference has the upper hand, fear and anger are triggered when we feel we might not get what we want.

It is of course natural to feel closer to friends and family, but the 'in group' does imply an 'out group'; there is a boundary, with others left outside in the cold. The notion of friendship is anyway a somewhat random and arbitrary process: someone who is our closest friend today may have been a stranger last year, and they may return to that status next year. In that sense, everyone in the world is potentially our best friend – we simply haven't got to know them yet. So operating from a place of preference is not actually logical.

We do feel empathy for strangers, but generally only when their suffering is obvious enough. Again, we feel connected, with empathy, only towards certain individuals or when people are in specific situations. As we walk down a busy street, the people rushing past us are simply nameless objects and we don't have any particular feeling for them. If one of them, however, especially a child or an elderly person, trips and falls, then we *do* feel something and hopefully we might reach out to help them. Sadly, they've had to present a strong enough case to trigger our empathy – it's almost as if people have to *buy* our empathy by *deserving it*, through exhibiting obvious symptoms. But this empathic response is short-sighted and is simply reactive. Until they fall over, are they not worthy objects of our love and kindness? Are they only suffering when they fall?

When we learn meditation, we become more aware of the human condition and we can begin to see that people's suffering is often hidden. Those walking down the street with unremarkable facial expressions are simply not showing the struggle they carry within themselves. Are we too not like that? Does it make sense to only feel kindness towards others when they *show* their pain?

Another aspect of preference is when we don't feel empathy for our 'enemies' or for those people we dislike. We feel angry with them, and of course we don't want to *condone* their behaviour. When we think of having empathy towards somebody who has done terrible things, it feels shocking and repellent, as it suggests we might be okay with what they did. So all we know to do in that situation is to close down our hearts.

Preference, then, in all its forms reduces empathy to a limited response, which is not that useful to anyone.

Frustration

The most painful characteristic of empathy is the sense of helplessness or *frustration*. Seeing so much suffering in the world around us can easily lead us to feel overwhelmed and frustrated, as we think we are unable to *do* anything about it. We are just stuck with feeling bad.

There are three common reactions to that frustration. Sometimes we become consumed by emotion. We cry and feel choked by overwhelming feelings; this is called 'empathic distress' and it can be incredibly debilitating. At other times we might become angry, where the frustration manifests as blame and rage. The third, most common, reaction is to become numb and cold. We simply don't know what to do about the problems of others, and so we shut down. This is the usual reaction when we walk past a homeless person on the street: we don't know what to do – we can't bear it – and so we look down and continue on our way.

COMPASSION IS THE KEY TO HAPPINESS

Empathy, despite its limitations, is a starting point and then compassion goes far deeper. Compassion means to understand others' pain, to cultivate the deep intention to help them, and then to translate that into action. It is like learning to swim so that we can rescue the drowning person, but it is also about helping others in a deeper, more sustainable way, not just through short-term relief.

Compassion has selfless, unconditional and limitless qualities. Where empathy is bound up with expectations and requirements, unconditional compassion implies 'no matter what'; it leads us to connect with others not 'because' or 'when', but to love them just as they are. Compassion is something we can develop through working on our minds. It expands our empathy beyond its limitations.

Research using brain imaging has shown that when somebody is experiencing compassion rather than just empathy, there is less activation of emotion and feeling, and more of *intention*; the brain's motor cortex is preparing for action. Researchers concluded that the brain resonance activated through empathy easily leads to debilitation and distress, while compassion can be seen as a trainable method, creating resilience and 'prosocial' behaviour. Prosocial behaviour is compassion in action; it means to get out there and do something for others.

We are talking here about a training of the heart. This is very different from experiencing random feelings of empathy which arise as a reaction to the suffering of others – feelings that can simply be a type of pity, or a drain on our resources. We can develop compassion as our core, our nature, our very being, rather than just experiencing an emotional reaction that switches itself on and off.

Love and compassion are emphasised at the heart of every spiritual tradition, and in meditation and mindfulness practices they play a central role, with techniques for the development of stable, unconditional, limitless love and compassion. It is only through cultivating these qualities that we can really help people, as well as find a happiness which is inseparable from the happiness of others. Happiness, like everything else, is an interdependent reality.

In meditation texts 'love' is described as 'loving kindness', which means the heartfelt wish for others to experience true happiness, and 'compassion' is the wish for others to be free from pain and suffering. But there is a further step: we can develop a commitment to help others learn how to create the causes for future happiness and how to be free from the causes for future suffering. The use of the word *'for'* rather than *'of'* is deliberate here, as when we say the 'causes *of* happiness/suffering', there is an assumption that it's the things around us that are the causes. When, on the other hand, we refer to the 'causes *for* happiness/suffering', we are acknowledging that we ourselves create those causes, through our thinking, which then lead to happiness or suffering. Understanding this means that liberation is possible.

If we can create a dynamic link between our meditation

practice and compassion, this will provide us with a clear path and direction. Compassion is the fastest path to happiness for ourselves and for the world around us. We explored in the previous chapter how the happiness of the individual is interlinked with that of the group; through training in compassion we can discover a happiness which is fully integrated within interdependence.

The important point here is to consider *why* we are meditating. If our meditation practice is driven by the demands of our ego, we simply get caught up in the cycle of grasping, where we crave and run after feelings of well-being, as described in Chapter Seven.

All suffering, without exception, is born from a mind which seeks happiness for oneself, whereas perfect, enduring happiness arises through a mind which seeks to benefit others.

– Buddhist proverb

This statement suggests that true happiness will only arise through compassion. The more we grasp after personal satisfaction, wanting to feel good, the more our expectations lead to disappointment and dissatisfaction. The compassionate mind, on the other hand, moves away from that grasping and enters a more spacious mentality, tapping into limitless freedom and unconditional happiness. Can we therefore meditate not just for ourselves but also for others?

HOW TO HELP OTHERS

As our meditation practice progresses, we become more aware of our own mental processes. We experience first-hand how unstable the mind can be – we see how it regularly goes to places we'd rather it didn't. We realise how difficult it is to control our thoughts and emotions and how easily reactivity can take over. As this growing insight provides us with a keener sensitivity towards our own minds, it guides us to a better understanding of others and their suffering. As we also discover how the habits of the mind can be *transformed*, we become better equipped to help others more effectively. We can start to connect more compassionately, and we can recognise our tendency to judge people – 'He's bad/She's bad/They should know better.' Instead of demonising a person whom we dislike, simply discarding them as wrong or even evil, we could acknowledge the pain and confusion which drive them. This understanding can be the key element which brings peace to all concerned.

Profound compassion therefore arises when we learn to accept the human condition with kindness. Through that deeper insight, we can be more helpful to others. Additionally, challenging relationships and situations can begin to transform.

As we've now seen, compassion is not just about feeling bad for others or being kind to them – it is more than that. It is about building a stable commitment to the happiness of all beings, which is a long-term approach rather than random moments of making others feel better. A metaphor for this is the training of a medical student. They want to help others, to improve and save lives, and so they need to go to medical school. During those years of study, they are not actually saving any lives, but they are accumulating the skills which they will later use when they qualify. Our meditation practice can be something like that. With this in mind, we know we are training in meditation so that we can help others.

Setting the intention

In practical terms, when you do even a short session of meditation, it is good to actively create a compassionate intention. This can be done at the beginning and end of the session, through spending a few moments mentally establishing the motivation for your meditation. You can think, 'I am doing this practice not only for myself, but also for others. Through this training, may I eventually be able to help others, in the deepest way possible.' Creating this aspiration through your thinking is incredibly powerful, as it sets the tone for the meditation, connects you with a deeper reason for meditating and invests its power in the most beneficial way. It gives you a plan, a purpose, transforming helpless feelings of empathy into the dynamic path of compassion training. This is reflected in the research findings which showed an activation of intention in the brain's motor cortex, as mentioned earlier (see p. 169). So we are not left simply feeling sorry for people, but instead we are training for sustainable and meaningful action.

Perhaps we cannot help many people right now, today, but we are accumulating skills which we can later use to make a difference. As our practice develops and our understanding of the mind deepens, we will accelerate our ability to help others to transform their suffering. As we cultivate peace in our own minds, we will be able to bring more of that to the world around us. This doesn't always mean teaching others how to meditate, and in fact it's only wise to do that if one is properly qualified – maybe that is something which will come later. Promoting happiness in others can be done in many ways. Every act of kindness and under-standing can have a ripple effect. We are all interrelated, which means our actions affect how somebody else will then treat the next person. That is how happiness can spread.

World peace must develop from inner peace. Peace is not just mere absence of violence. Peace is, I think, the manifestation of human compassion.
— His Holiness the 14th Dalai Lama

THREE LEVELS OF COMPASSION

As our practice matures, we will progress through three stages of compassion development:

1. Viewing everybody as equal
2. Seeing the needs of others as more important than our own
3. Altruism: taking on the burden of others

1. Viewing everybody as equal
The first level of compassion is where we acknowledge that nobody is more important than anyone else, we are

all equal. This equanimity is the basis for compassion development, as it puts our ego in perspective. We tend to place ourselves at the centre of everything and that ego fixation, in its extreme form, can lead to either arrogance or self-hatred ('There's nobody quite as bad as me, I'm just the worst').

Everybody in this world wants the same thing – happiness and freedom from suffering. We are all together on one path. There isn't really any difference between us – on the surface we have varied lifestyles, but our underlying aim is the same; it's a level playing field, with a shared goal. If we stand back and think about this, it creates a feeling of togetherness, of community. Normally when we meet a stranger, we feel disconnected, but as soon as we realise that we have something in common with them, we feel a connection and our attitude changes. Through this first stage of compassion we can experience a sense of working in unity towards the same aim. Here we are recognising the power of interdependence.

2. Seeing the needs of others as more important than our own

The second stage, when our practice has matured a little, is to put others first, to see them as more important than ourselves. This, of course, has to be backed up by strong meditation training, otherwise we could end up with the mentality of being a 'doormat' or a martyr – 'I'm going to be miserable and let everyone else be happy. I'm just rubbish.' Actually the doormat is a strongly suppressed ego; we are lying under that heavy doormat silently screaming. Through meditation training, however, we can start to let go of our habit of solidifying the self and instead begin to discover a spacious mind that clings less to self-centred thoughts.

Others really *are* more important than us; numerically speaking this is true – there is only one of us and there are billions of others. If there were two groups, with group A containing simply us, one person, and group B containing all other life forms, and we were to ask the question, 'If the needs of one group should come second to the needs of the other, which way around should it be?' the answer is obvious. Our lives do work according to this principle; if there are ten of us sitting in a room and nine people want the heating turned up and one person wants it turned down, we vote – we decide according to the majority wish or need. In spite of this, however, our tendency is to live our lives as Number One, which just leads to stress and dissatisfaction – as previously explored.

3. Altruism: taking on the burden of others

The third and highest level of compassion is altruism, which means to willingly take the burden of others upon ourselves. Again, this doesn't mean being a martyr or a doormat – it is a deep commitment to care for others, and then to do something about that. We naturally have this attitude in relation to our loved ones; for example, if we had a child who became unwell and we could somehow take that sickness upon ourselves and free them from it, we would do so in a heartbeat. If we were walking up a hill, and we saw our aged mother next to us, bent over and struggling, carrying a heavy bag, would we not readily take the bag from her to free her? This is a natural impulse in relation to those we love, and the highest stage of compassion training is to extend that attitude to all beings.

What would it mean to take on the burden of all beings? It means to cultivate a greater awareness of the human condition and a wish to help others, leading to a strong commitment to train in meditation for that purpose. Meditation then translates into action, benefitting others.

Many Buddhist texts use the love between mother and child as imagery for compassion. The supreme qualities of the mother are nurturing and unconditional acceptance. For compassion training, it's sometimes helpful to think of ourselves as everyone's mother. At other times it's helpful to see others as our mother. This can give rise to loving care and sincere gratitude; it also helps to establish a more selfless, altruistic wish to help others.

As we saw in the previous chapter, all things are linked and connected, which means that everything and everybody depends on others. All the objects we use, such as our food and clothing, have been made for us by others. Because of interdependence, *everyone* has been part of the creation of those things. When we eat something as simple as a sandwich, there have been so many factors involved in getting it to our plates; people laboured in the fields and worked in the packaging, transportation and selling of the goods. In fact, everybody on this planet has in some way been indirectly related to the process, as everything depends on everything else, even down to the air we breathe. How is it possible for the shop to sell us the bread? The society around us keeps the economy going through people's everyday actions, so in fact everyone has in some way fed us, just as a mother nurtures her baby. If everybody, even unknowingly and indirectly, has supported our lives, we owe them a huge debt of gratitude, which will arise naturally if we train ourselves in the mode of thinking presented above. In the same way that we would jump up to protect our mother if she were suffering, we can nurture in ourselves a deep wish to care for all living beings. That feeling becomes the basis for building a sense of universal compassion.

COMPASSION TRAINING

In addition to establishing a compassionate motivation for our meditation sessions, as described on page 173, the key to compassion training is in how we treat our own minds. Meditation practice activates a compassionate attitude towards our thoughts and emotions. Compassion is all about unconditional love, which means to love someone or something just the way they are – we don't wish to change them or want them to be different, they are perfect just as they are. Can we do that with our thoughts and emotions?

Normally we have a habit of either pushing away our thoughts or trying to develop them into more thoughts – elaborating one thought into two, three, maybe four thoughts and so on. We do this with emotions too. This elaboration is in fact a form of aggression, just like the pushing away; we are basically saying that this thought or emotion is not good enough the way it is, we'd like to have more of it, we need it to develop into a further story. It's as if somebody gives us a cake and we then insist they put candles on top and sparklers, and decorate the plate. The message is that this cake isn't enough; we want a bigger cake, with glitter and icing.

We do that with a thought or an emotion; we can't just leave it the way it is, we want to take it on a journey to make it more interesting, or we want to push it away. Within meditation practice, however, we are learning a total acceptance of everything that arises in our minds, not judging things as good or bad, but simply letting it all be and returning to the meditation focus. This non-judgemental attitude is the foundation for having compassion towards oneself and others. It is the only way to find genuine, lasting happiness.

In this way, even a simple practice such as mindful breathing can be the key that unlocks compassion. Additionally, there are some more specific compassion techniques below.

MEDITATION EXERCISES

How do we develop a strong commitment to compassion training? Perhaps it's good to address that little voice within which constantly asks, 'What's in it for me?' The first exercise helps us realise that compassion development benefits us too.

1. Thinking about compassion

This meditation exercise uses 'contemplation' or 'analytical meditation': you'll be engaging with your thinking in order to activate deeper wisdom. Earlier in this chapter we looked at the difference between empathy and compassion; this exercise compares selfishness with compassion. You're going to internally ask yourself a series of questions and explore the answers that come up. This is about not jumping to conclusions, but simply thinking and discovering.

Sit in a quiet place, with a good posture (see p. 70). When doing contemplation exercises it is okay to close your eyes if you prefer.

Begin the session by becoming aware of your body; feel its contact with the chair. Then focus on your shoulders and finally the feeling of the ground under your feet. This is done to anchor your attention in the present moment.

After a few moments, think about selfishness and mentally ask yourself the following five questions, spending a few minutes on each one and exploring the answers which come up in your mind.

1 *When I am selfish, very wrapped up in myself, how does that feel? Does my mind feel big or small? Relaxed or tight? Is there perhaps a sense of worry, a need to run after, protect and hold on to things?*

2 *How do my problems feel when I am being selfish? Do they feel bigger or smaller? Am I putting my problems and concerns under a microscope and do they now seem more intense; do I lose perspective?*

3 *What effect does a selfish mind have on the environment around me?*

You could look at this third question first at a global level and then the more personal. Is it not self-centred thinking that has had such a detrimental effect on our planet's ecology, on societies, communities and families? The irony is that those who are destroying the planet are not considering that it is their very own grandchildren and great-grandchildren who will suffer as a result; and even though those individuals might not yet have been born, they would of course see them as family, their loved ones. At a personal level, the main factor causing problems in families and other relationships is when people only think of themselves and act in a short-sighted manner, which inevitably causes conflict to arise.

4 *What feedback do I get as a result of my selfish thinking and behaviour?*

Isn't it true that people don't really like selfish people? People love to be around kind people, who are less self-obsessed.

5 *As a result of that, how do I end up feeling about myself? Do I fall into a sense of loneliness?*

After completing these five questions, the second part of the exercise is to apply the same questions when thinking about the qualities of a compassionate mind, which is the mentality with less self-interest, more open-ness to others, a greater sense of generosity and a wish to help people. Begin by thinking of those qualities, and then turn your mind to the questions:

1 *How does that type of mind feel?*

2 *How do my problems feel when I am in a compassionate mind state?*

3 *What is the effect on the environment, society and relationships?*

4 *What sort of feedback do I get from others?*

5 *How does that make me feel about myself?*

What you might discover is that the compassionate mind feels more spacious, less tight and not so self-absorbed. Problems feel smaller, as you put them into perspective, seeing how *others* suffer too and that you are not the only one. You can gain more objectivity when you remove your pain from under the microscope and become more interested in the happiness of others and how to improve that. In many ways, our problems have a lot to do with how much we obsessively dwell on them.

When you are kind and compassionate, the feedback you get from others is usually positive – people love to be around you, and you feel a sense of connection. Compassion is therefore a 'win–win' situation.

This session can be timed at 15 or 20 minutes. The exercise helps you to understand the importance of kindness and compassion from a deep internal perspective. We all just want to be happy, but until now we've perhaps not grasped that this is only possible through giving rise to genuine compassion. You could begin to realise that compassion development is good for others and also good for you. Living from a place of ego is a 'lose–lose' game where ultimately nobody is happy.

2. Compassion meditation

Sit in a quiet place, adopting the formal posture for meditation, as described on p. 70.

First, generate the motivation that you're going to meditate not only for your own benefit, but also for the benefit of others. Spend a moment setting this intention.

Become aware of your body; feel its contact with the chair, and then be aware of your shoulders. After that, feel the ground under your feet, just for a few moments.

You're going to be using visualisation, which means to create a mental image. Imagine that in the centre of your chest, level with your heart but in the middle, there is a glowing ball of light. It can be whatever colour you like; I find white or pink helpful. Think that this light represents the deep bliss and freedom which are your true nature, your deeper mind, as described in Chapter Two. Its qualities are limitless unconditional love and compassion.

Imagine that the ball of light is glowing and radiating rays of light, which start to fill up your body. As the light emanates inside you, feel as if you are being bathed in love, kindness and happiness from within. All traces of pain and suffering dissolve.

Then the light radiates out of your body and reaches out to others. Generate a deep wish that others may find happiness and freedom from suffering, and that they will discover how to create the *causes* for happiness and freedom.

Begin that process by focusing on somebody you feel close to and for whom you have a great deal of love.

You are mentally sending them kindness and happiness, and as you do that, imagine that the rays of light from your heart are radiating towards them, filling them up. All their problems, and whatever prevents them from experiencing genuine happiness, melt away as the light fills their body.

Next extend that wish to your family and friends. Again, the light from you radiates out to them, filling them up.

Then send that same wish, for happiness and freedom from suffering, to acquaintances and then to strangers. The light rays reach out to them too, filling them with peace and freedom.

The next step, if you feel comfortable doing so, is to do the same for people you find difficult. As the light fills those people, it removes their harmful intentions and dissolves all conflict, like warm sunlight melting ice or frost.

Spend a few minutes on each step, and at the end of the sequence, wish the same – complete happiness and freedom from suffering – for absolutely everybody. At this stage imagine that the light is spilling out of your body in all directions, filling the universe with love and happiness.

As you draw close to the end of your session, let go of the visualisation of light, and spend a few moments allowing the mind to relax in a feeling of kindness, happiness and freedom.

The last step is to take a few moments to mentally dedicate your meditation training to the happiness of all beings. You are reminding yourself of the deeper reason for meditating, which is to eventually be able to help others in the fullest way possible.

As usual, the session can take 10 or 15 minutes, or whatever length of time you wish to practise for.

CHAPTER TEN

Forgiveness

● ● ●

One of our greatest obstacles to happiness is when we feel resentment towards other people. Sometimes we've been hurt, and we carry a wound within us; at other times it's the daily grind of feeling irritated by the words and actions of others. Either way, other people often seem to 'do our heads in'.

> *L'enfer, c'est les autres. (Hell is other people.)*
>
> – Jean-Paul Sartre

As an actor I once appeared in Sartre's famous play *Huis Clos* (*Vicious Circle* or *No Exit*), in which the characters are sent to hell, only to discover that it is a very comfortable Regency-style drawing room containing two other people. The three of them spend the entire play mentally tormenting each other. For me, being in this play was a particular kind of hell, as I had not learned my lines properly and each night felt like falling out of a plane with no parachute. At the end of the play, the characters, who have been driving one another mad, try to kill each other, but then realise they cannot as they are already dead, and so they laugh grimly; I then had the line, 'Oh well, let's continue.'

Is hell other people? Surely being caught up in a cycle of anger and revenge is the true hell; it's like burning in a fiery pit. Only when we can forgive others, as well as ourselves, can we be truly happy, otherwise we are constantly weighed down by a painful burden.

Anger and fear can make us deeply unhappy: we become consumed by negativity, which even undermines our immune systems. Carrying that resentment is like holding on to a hot coal; the more we hold on to it, the more it burns us. Wouldn't we rather put it down and be free?

What stops us from putting down that burden of hurt? It is our attachment to our internal habits: the strong mental 'glue'. As we progress on the path of meditation, we could start to discover the freedom of being able to let go and move on. This requires regular practice, to help 'thin down' that grasping mentality. In practical terms, every time the mind wanders during meditation and we gently bring our attention back to the support – the breath, for example – we are building that skill of letting go.

In the previous chapter we explored the need for developing compassion. It is easy, however, to feel compassion for the weak and vulnerable, but when it comes to our 'enemies' this is when we truly get tested, and that's where it really counts. When we can forgive those who have hurt us, as well as those who simply irritate us, *then* our compassion has been developed in a stable manner. Until then it is partial.

RECOGNISE THE ANGER

As well as practising regular meditation to loosen up our mental attachment, we can take a series of intelligent steps in our thinking, which will more quickly free us from resentment. The first step is to ask: who is the real enemy? Is it the person 'out there' or is it our *reaction* to them? Instead of remaining stuck in our perpetual stories of how terrible that person is and ruminating over all the things they have said or done, we could instead examine our habits of mental reactivity. We can look at the anger itself. When we do this, it opens up the possibility for change. Our true enemies are the anger and pain that we carry inside us, and those are what really damage us.

RADICAL GRATITUDE

The fastest path to enlightenment is for people to insult you.

– Akong Tulku Rinpoche

The next step is to realise that the hurtful situation can actually benefit our training in compassion. We've been presented with an opportunity to develop the skill of forgiveness, which is a high form of compassion. We might now begin to feel *grateful* towards the so-called enemy. This attitude in itself *is* forgiveness, as we now see that person as a support for our training. If we are really committed to the path of developing compassion, then we do need people in our lives who will test that. Perhaps, then, our enemies are our best friends.

In general, our friends don't help us to develop our minds as much as our enemies do. Our interactions with friends don't usually test us and get us to work on ourselves, whereas our enemies can push our buttons and show us where we are stuck. We generally have friends because we like being around people who make us feel comfortable, however it is the challenging, disruptive elements in our lives which truly help us to grow. How would we learn the life-changing skill of forgiveness without them?

The things which normally bring up resistance in us are the very things that make us stronger – just as when we go to a gym, we need to lift weights in order to build muscle. As I mentioned in Chapter Six, on building habits, an effective method for training in resilience is to mindfully relax when you're standing in a queue, are stuck in traffic or whenever you feel tension or discomfort in your body. This kind of training produces deep benefits, as you're reprogramming the usual tendency of pushing things away – the habit of rejecting discomfort. From a deeper perspective, in the same way that a traffic jam can help us to grow, so too can our worst enemy.

DEEPER UNDERSTANDING

The next step is to try to understand the internal suffering and confusion of the person who hurt us. When someone does or says something that causes us to feel harmed, we mainly suffer because we assume it was deliberate, that they 'meant' it.

In life we generally differentiate between what is done by accident and what is deliberate. If someone accidentally steps on our foot, we don't really mind, but if they march up to us, stare us in the eyes and then stamp down on our foot, it's war.

A more truthful perspective can be to see both situations in the same light – in both scenarios nothing is 'deliberate', as in each case the other person is not fully in control of themselves. They are out of balance, driven by negative impulses, and they are coming from a place of stress and misery. When somebody is gripped by their negativity, they do and say things which they wouldn't if they were happy and in a state of balance. Forgiveness training involves understanding where the aggressor is really coming from; the aggressor comes from aggression itself, and that internal state of mind is something which is very hard for them to control.

This can dawn on us if we take a really honest look at ourselves. Are we in control of ourselves 100 per cent of the time? We sometimes become stressed and unhappy, and then do and say things that we don't really mean, and which we later regret. How many times have we thought or said, '*Why* did I do/say that?' That is not the talk of somebody who is in control of themselves. When we are upset, do we *plan* to be upset? When we are angry, is that a deliberate choice?

When a person is filled with negativity it's like eating poison and then unstoppably throwing up. In the same way, when somebody is angry or suffering in some way, the poison comes out in words and deeds, often uncontrollably. Feeling overpowered by anger and pain is very much like being under the influence of alcohol, where one's actions often become regrettable.

How do we *know* what level of suffering the other person is experiencing? How do we know about their background, their childhood, or even what might have happened to them yesterday? These will all be contributing factors to how they are feeling and behaving in the present moment. We often use the phrase 'they should know better', which is actually ridiculous, as how can anyone know what they don't know? They are simply who they are in this moment, knowing what they know. Again, are we ourselves always fully in control?

Imagine the example of a mother whose baby is delirious with a high fever. As she tries to comfort and feed her child, the baby is kicking and screaming, but she knows her child is unwell and so she feels compassion rather than taking things personally and feeling hurt or attacked. She knows her baby is in the grip of a fever and is therefore out of control. She forgives and wants nothing other than to help her child. In the same way, people are often overwhelmed by their confusion and negativity, and they lash out. That confusion is just like a high fever; it takes over. Rarely, however, do we realise or acknowledge this fact in the person who treats us badly, and instead we think that they're 'out to get us'. It might even feel as if they had some kind of master plan to destroy us.

Even in a case where someone *does* seem to plan their actions, maybe in a seemingly cold-blooded manner, or they appear to *enjoy* hurting others, that person is still not in control of themselves – they are under the power of strong internal negativity. If we can recognise this aspect of the human condition it can be incredibly liberating, as the burden of rage and indignation will start to drop away.

We are sometimes in a situation where somebody has been behaving in a negative way, perhaps speaking irritably to us or to others, and then we find out that something horrible recently happened to them. We immediately drop our anger as we understand that they are unhappy and that's what is now spilling out of them. However, isn't every situation like that? We don't need to wait to be given the information. We can instead assume that there will always be something in the near or distant past which has led the other person to this point. Instead of blaming the person, we could blame their negative emotions. We could be angry with anger, not the human – they are simply being thrown about by that anger. If we follow this line of thinking, revenge is illogical and unhelpful; travelling that path simply perpetuates the cycle of negativity.

Would this attitude make us into a passive 'doormat', allowing everybody to abuse us, simply turning the other cheek? No, it would not, and although there will be situations where we do need to stand up for ourselves, we don't need to then walk away with toxic anger and hurt festering within us.

What usually holds us back from forgiving is that we fear it means somehow condoning the actions of others – 'letting them get away with it', making us into a victim. Perhaps we see forgiveness as a weakness rather than a strength. But in truth, they *have* 'got away with it' if we *don't* forgive, as we are now perpetually in pain. If, on the other hand, we train in forgiveness, then the very things which have hurt us have become the greatest aids to our journey of meditation, making us stronger. So everybody wins.

> *La liberté est ce que vous faites avec ce qui a été fait à vous.*
> *(Freedom is what you do with what's been done to you.)*
>
> – Jean-Paul Sartre

MENTAL CONFLICT

We have a love–hate relationship with our own thoughts and emotions. We either chase them or try to get rid of them. When we are meditating and we realise our minds have wandered, we often feel we've somehow failed, and we start to mentally beat ourselves up over it, as described earlier. We could even begin to hate our thoughts – we feel we need to shoot them down with some kind of gun, which makes us sit there in a state of tension. Through this attitude, the more we meditate, the more stressed we end up.

True forgiveness is developed through learning to accept whatever is happening in the mind. This is a deep form of unconditional love, and it is the key to forgiving ourselves and others.

In meditation all we need to do is notice that our minds have wandered, and then return our attention to the object of meditation – such as the breath. Training in this way makes us stronger. To learn that, we need to have somewhere to return *from*, and so the wandering mind has in fact helped us – the thoughts are aids to the meditation, not enemies. This attitude – a non-judgemental acceptance towards our thoughts and emotions, resolving our internal mental conflict – becomes the foundation for the development of forgiveness. If we can forgive our thoughts, we can forgive ourselves, and forgive our enemies.

FORGIVING OURSELVES

Many people struggle with habits of self-loathing. We can find it hard to forgive ourselves, perhaps for specific things we have done, or we may feel a general sense of disgust at our own shortcomings.

I think there are elements within modern culture that encourage this problem. We are constantly fed messages through advertising which tell us that we cannot possibly be okay with the way we are – we must strive to look, be and feel better, and to have more. Advertising plays on our insecurities as well as our desires. As I described earlier, in a world of grasping we constantly create feelings of lack and dissatisfaction. We also live in times where the old habit of 'curtain twitching' has become digitalised, and it is now global and highly addictive. It is no surprise that we inhabit a culture of insecurity; everybody is judging everyone else.

Our striving to be perfect, and the constant exposure to imagery of so-called perfection, can cause us to feel quite bad about ourselves. It is no wonder, then, that when we make a mistake or we perceive our own shortcomings, we fall into habits of self-loathing. We have internalised those judgements which are all around us.

Some people are tormented by guilt and self-hatred. I used to have a persistent, self-condemning internal monologue, as well as patterns of highly self-destructive behaviour. I would find my own company very difficult, even distasteful. If people appeared to like me, I would assume there must be something wrong with them, as I felt so unlikeable. This led me into numerous destructive relationships and situations. When I became a monk and went into that first nine-month retreat, the harsh internal voice telling me that I was rubbish, bad, even evil, intensified, and I would often hold my head in my hands begging it to stop. I now realise that this came from a huge amount of tension; when we are stressed, our main negative habit tends to be accentuated. I was meditating in quite a harsh manner, sometimes doing seven-hour sessions and not stopping until I felt I had done it 'well enough'; it was a tense and miserable time. Things shifted during my longer retreat of four years, when I learned how to give some compassion to that part of myself. I would feel as if a knife was twisting in my heart, an agonising feeling. When I started to give love and kindness to the sensation itself, everything changed. At the end of this chapter there will be an exercise that relates to this. The benefit for me has been that I now find it much easier to forgive myself. I am no longer hard on myself, in fact very gentle. Sometimes this can veer into being a bit lazy, but on the whole it has helped me to be a much happier person.

Steps for self-forgiveness

We can apply the same three steps that were described earlier in this chapter: recognition, gratitude and understanding.

Recognition means to calmly acknowledge our mistakes or our negativity; we can do this without falling into guilt. It is good to tap into the knowledge described in Chapter Two, that deep down we are ultimately happy, good and pure. Our negativity is simply like dust – it can be cleaned away through meditation training.

Gratitude means to appreciate that we have seen something in ourselves that we can work on, and so there is an opportunity. Once we can see that our problems provide a chance for training in resilience, our attitude to them can become one of gratitude.

Understanding means to see our shortcomings as part of the human condition. There is nothing wrong with us, we simply have minds that haven't yet been trained, and so of course we are liable to make mistakes. If we can each see ourselves as a 'work in progress', that will help us develop self-forgiveness.

These three ways of thinking need to be combined with regular meditation practice, which will enable us to be less controlled by our habits of mentally beating ourselves up.

It is also helpful to remember that everything changes; nothing is fixed, solid or unchanging. These problems that we might be currently fixating upon, will one day be a memory, and as we keep practising meditation we are going to improve. We have a habit of forgetting impermanence, and so when something goes wrong it becomes easy to think we are doomed.

FORGIVING LIFE'S CHALLENGES

Up to now we've been exploring forgiveness towards others and ourselves. We can also learn how to be patient with difficult events. A powerful type of forgiveness is to transform our attitudes to life's challenges. The key to this is to use mindfulness to stay fully present with an unpleasant experience, learning to abandon judgement.

I told a story earlier in which I was standing on a hot, crowded, underground train in London. I managed to practise mindfulness, wholeheartedly accepting that present moment. Everything changed when I stopped fighting the situation and began to use it as practice. I focused on physical sensations, without trying to push them away; this diverted my attention from the negative thinking – which itself goes away when we are no longer feeding it. If we can be fully present with discomfort, we discover a profound acceptance, which includes a sense of joy, as resistance drops away and we feel that sense of freedom.

We are often engaged in some form of argument with reality, where we are wishing for a different moment. However, even if we're sick or in pain, we can learn to remove the filter of resistance; we are moving past those distracting thoughts of 'I don't like this', and we are going directly to what is actually happening – embracing the moment without judgement. This is how to live a life with no filters. It doesn't mean that we would never take medicines or seek to improve things; it simply means to joyfully accept what cannot be changed. If we realise that this moment, however it may be, is beautiful just the way it is, then we are truly choosing happiness.

I remember once walking with my teacher Akong Rinpoche in London. We were visiting our monastery's branch there and we had a break from the teaching sessions. We took a stroll along the Thames's South Bank. It was an exceptionally beautiful sunny day and I was in heaven, walking in the sunshine with my favourite person. When we were alone like this we would simply hang out and be casual with each other – there was no formality. I turned to Rinpoche and said, 'It's really beautiful, isn't it?' Somehow right at the moment I finished speaking those words, we entered a dark tunnel with graffiti all over the walls and the smell of urine; I think there was even a pool of vomit on the ground, it was just hideous. Rinpoche simply said, 'For me everything is beautiful.' I imagine that for somebody whose mind contains no habits of resistance or fear, *everything* must look and feel great. *That* is true happiness, and such a person is invincible.

MEDITATION EXERCISES

It is easier to begin by training in forgiving life's challenges. This lays the foundation for being able to forgive people.

1. Resilience

Sit in a quiet place, adopting the formal posture for meditation, as previously explained (see p. 70).

Spend a moment generating the wish to develop stronger compassion for yourself and others; you're dedicating your meditation journey to that aim.

Become aware of your body; feel its contact with the chair, and then sense the ground under your feet, just for a few moments.

Next, notice if there is a place in your body where you feel some discomfort; or perhaps your mind is experiencing a particular feeling or mood – find where in your body you can feel that emotion resonating. Perhaps it's a sensation in your chest or lower abdomen.

Now that you've located the discomfort or the feeling of your emotion, focus on that sensation with a sense of loving awareness. This means that you are present, with total acceptance and even an emotional warmth towards what you are focusing on. Try to completely accept the sensation, to mentally embrace it. Relax your attention very deeply *into* that place of tension, as if you are 'becoming one' with it. In this way, you are bathing the area with compassion.

Spend most of the session in this way. Of course your mind will wander; when you realise that you got lost in thoughts or other distractions, gently bring your attention back to the sensation and the feeling of acceptance.

If at any point during the session you feel overwhelmed, don't force yourself. Simply back off for a while by focusing on your body in general, or on your breathing (without trying to breathe deeply or in any special way).

When you are ready to end the session, spend a few moments mentally dedicating your meditation training to the happiness of all beings.

This session can take 10 or 15 minutes, or whatever length of time you wish to practise for.

2. Forgiving others

Sit with a good posture as usual. Begin your session by establishing the compassionate motivation to meditate for the benefit of yourself and others.

Spend a few moments settling into the present moment; you can use your body as the focus, feeling its contact with the chair and the floor.

Bring to mind a difficult relationship, or somebody about whom you have negative feelings. Think about the person and allow whatever feelings that arise simply to be there.

As explained earlier, the three steps for forgiveness are recognition, gratitude and understanding.

i) **Recognition.** Recognise that it is your anger, pain or irritation that are the true enemies here. It is those feelings that are making you suffer right now in this moment. Don't condemn those feelings; the point of this part of the exercise is to see that the enemy is within and the way that you deal with your emotions *is* something you can change.

ii) **Gratitude.** Reflect upon the fact that the person who has hurt you, or whom you dislike, is giving you an opportunity to learn forgiveness. They are a catalyst for your path. You could feel a kind of gratitude towards them. Thinking like this helps to reframe the situation as something helpful rather than harmful.

iii) **Understanding.** Think about the other person's suffering or confusion, and how that negativity controls them from within, making them do or say things which cause problems.

To take this understanding to a deeper level, spend a few minutes imagining that you are that person – imagine yourself in their skin, walking in their shoes. Try to mentally inhabit their reality and appreciate how it might feel to be driven by such negativity and confusion. Sit for a while simply breathing as that person, imagining how they might feel.

This exercise can help us begin to forgive, as we are

feeling the imagined experience of *their* perspective – thus moving away from a one-sided viewpoint.

If at any point during the exercise you feel overwhelmed or distressed, don't force yourself to continue; simply rest by focusing on your body, and perhaps at this point switch to the first practice in this chapter, the 'resilience' exercise.

When your session time is up – usually 10 or 15 minutes – focus on your body for a few moments, simply being aware of your sitting position and then feeling the ground under your feet.

End the session by spending a few moments mentally dedicating your meditation training to the happiness of all beings, cultivating the deep wish that we may all forgive each other and find freedom from resentment and pain.

CHAPTER ELEVEN
Energising Your Practice

● ● ●

Kagyu Samye Ling Monastery in Scotland is an incredibly beautiful place. When I arrived there, the first thing that struck me was the wildness of the river at the end of the gardens, also the trees and the sense of space. I had come there from the frantic environment of New York – they call it the 'city that never sleeps', and it certainly buzzed with a pulsating energy – but I came to Scotland to be energised in a completely different way.

Hidden within the gentle hills of the Scottish Borders, Samye Ling's monastic complex has been designed in traditional Tibetan style and is surrounded by the beauty of nature. My favourite part of the gardens is a pond with a little island that you reach by crossing an arched wooden bridge. You can sit there on a bench watching the ducks. There is a palpable sense of calm in the air. People come to Samye Ling from across the globe to discover a place of peace and inspiration, with many seeking instruction in meditation – we often have a large number of guests attending courses. It can be enormously enriching to get out of the city, to go somewhere quiet with clean air and a pure environment, and to find fresh motivation through studying the mind.

These days I spend most of my time away from the monastery teaching, which takes me to many parts of the world. I give meditation classes in a lot of different environments, which means time spent in busy cities such as London, often living out of a suitcase. Under the guidance of my Abbot, I also look after some meditation centres in the UK – branches of the monastery – and we are working to open others. Some of these centres are in the middle of cities, where we've created tranquil places open to everybody, regardless of religious belief. People come there to learn compassion-based meditation practices, and we also provide spaces for complementary therapies and yoga.

Through working with meditation centres, I had to dive into the world of renovating old buildings, which meant learning about fundraising and construction projects. I have always believed that nothing should ever hold us back from fulfilling our wish to help others, and these projects started from the ground up; they were very hard work to get going, but they are now thriving and, I hope, helpful for many people.

My schedule is quite extreme and I do get tired, but I find that regular meditation gives me energy. Additionally, dropping into those small mindful moments several times per day is incredibly refreshing and balancing. I wouldn't dream of going for a single day without meditating; it feels as important to me as eating. I acknowledge that the discipline of being a monk makes it easier for me, but I am keen to help everybody – with their busy lives – learn how they can establish a routine of daily practice. When you discover how to do this, your life really does change.

MOTIVATION: LOSING IT AND FINDING IT

The old joke about meditators is that they're either busy meditating or feeling guilty about not meditating. Many people struggle to remain consistent in keeping up their practice every day, and then start to feel bad because they feel they 'should' be meditating, as they know it's good for them. They are aware that they are holding keys to freedom and happiness, but still catch themselves looking elsewhere. Feeling like a failure because of that can lead to a downward spiral of negativity, making it harder to get back into the habit of regular practice.

Our practice slips when life takes over. We become busy, and meditation becomes another thing on the list of 'shoulds'. We all know we should eat healthy food and take regular exercise; we try so hard to be good, and then before we know it, our plans have collapsed and we've demolished an entire packet of biscuits. We don't always look after ourselves very well, which is sometimes a form of self-loathing – maybe we feel we're not really worth it, so why bother? But we can transform this problem.

There are three main ways in which we lose energy for our practice, and for each of them there are effective remedies.

1. Lack of confidence
2. Procrastination
3. Being too busy

1. Lack of confidence

This is a habit of thinking that we don't really have what it takes, so we may as well not even try. We feel insecure about our ability to meditate; we think it's too difficult for us. This mindset prevents us from living our full potential, and instead we remain in the shadows of who we could be.

To remedy this lack of confidence, we can energise our minds by training ourselves to think about the enormous potential a human being possesses – we all have huge capacity. This has nothing to do with education or social position; it is simply our engineering: a person can learn the steps required to achieve long-term goals, and they can then apply those steps. That human capacity puts us in a very fortunate position on the planet: we can have significant effects on our surroundings, both positive and negative; and we can practise compassion to genuinely benefit others, thus using our lives in a highly positive way. Thinking about this can inspire us to see that we do actually have what it takes.

There is a second, deeper type of potential that we all have, which we could also reflect upon. Everybody has the capacity for mental transformation, and deep down we are hard-wired for happiness, as explained in Chapter Two. A part of us knows this; every time we sit down to meditate, we are in fact acknowledging that potential. Why else would we do something unless we know we have it in us to achieve its results?

Regularly reflecting on these two points – human capacity and our deeper potential for transformation – can help to foster true confidence.

2. Procrastination

The second obstacle to our practice is the habit of procrastination, putting things off till later: 'I'm really going to get into meditation tomorrow.' Tomorrow itself becomes a habit and so it never really comes, as we keep delaying. The remedy for this is to think more deeply about impermanence.

We tend to waste time because we think we have lots of it; we are not fully conscious of its passing. It is funny how a middle-aged person can still think like a 20-year-old: 'What shall I do when I grow up?' We feel as if we have the same length of time in front of us as we had in our 20s.

We can be quite deluded about the nature of reality; intellectually, we know that everything changes, that time is short and life doesn't go on forever; but we push that knowledge aside and tend to live as if we are immortal. People use the phrase 'if I die', as if there are options. Sometimes an event such as a serious illness or bereavement wakes us up to how precious our time is. We can, however, wake ourselves up by thinking more clearly.

Through deep reflection on how everything is impermanent, we can get more in touch with the reality of things. This will help us to appreciate our time better. It might seem that this sort of thinking would lead to hopelessness and despair, but we are cultivating this understanding within the context of thinking about limitless human potential and the power of meditation and mental transformation. Reflecting on impermanence within that framework will simply give us greater impetus to practise meditation more diligently.

3. Being too busy

Another distraction from meditation is when we become so busy with life, that there's just no time or space left. This is the most common obstacle in modern society; it's the laziness of busyness. We live in an era where being overloaded has become the norm, and we tend to rush about filling each moment with activity. Even when we are lying down we might perch our laptops on our stomachs and watch hours of television.

Of course, people need to work and look after their

families and friends, but all the extra things we do in the name of relaxation seem to leave us with little or no time or energy for meditation. To relax, people tend to throw themselves about in a darkened room (nightclub), rush around shopping, climb mountains or slouch on the sofa with their minds in a slightly burned-out state. We think we are relaxing, but *are* we really?

Perhaps we are settling for small hits of relaxation that depend entirely on specific triggers. Meditation, on the other hand, provides a deep, lasting peace rather than the dopamine hit that leaves us hungry for more.

The remedy for this third obstacle is to think about life from a different perspective. We could examine what we do with our time and what we're trying to achieve. We could question our attitudes around happiness – what is it and where does it come from? If happiness is a mental experience, surely the best investment would be to spend time training the mind?

ASKING THE RIGHT QUESTIONS

A good way to stay motivated is to regularly think about the importance of meditation. This will help us to understand its benefits, so that we'll feel more naturally inclined to practise. We can do this by asking ourselves a series of questions. This helps to increase our motivation and can be a lifeline if our practice has fallen apart and needs resurrecting.

The first question to explore is: *Why do I do all the things I do? What do I really want to achieve?*
Our main goal in life is to find stable, lasting happiness and to avoid suffering – that aim is behind everything we do. Even people who seem to enjoy misery are actually involved in a perverse search for happiness. People have different lifestyles, but the underlying motivations are identical: the CEO and the monk are both searching for the same thing – freedom and happiness – they just have different ways of going about it.

The second question is: *What am I doing about it?*
What are we *doing* to obtain happiness and to avoid discomfort? We could start to examine our activities. A powerful type of mindfulness is simply to observe ourselves during the span of a day, to see the things we do and to realise that they all come from that search for happiness.

The third question: *Is it working?*
An honest answer would be, 'Yes, sometimes, but it never

seems to last.' There's always something else that we seem to need, or something lurking around the corner to come and take it all away. Life never feels completely settled or secure.

The fourth question: *What are the* true *causes of happiness and suffering?*
It's not things, it's our *thoughts* about things. 'Things' don't have true independent existence anyway. We are having a mental experience of reality; the things we experience are not outside of or separate from our awareness of them.

Everything is down to perception. Imagine you are standing at the side of a pond: you're looking at the water and of course you would call that a pond. But is it really a pond? What if you were a fish inside that water? A fish swimming in the water would perceive that pond as the air that it breathes, and in fact that fish has no concept of anything outside – it's actually its entire universe. Who is 'right'? What if the fish and the human could hold a conversation? The human would say, 'It's a pond', and the fish would say, 'No, stupid, it's the *whole world*.' Are we not just living in perceived realities according to our mental conditioning?

If we view things in that light, where everything is a

projection of the mind, then we might have a different attitude towards happiness and suffering. It is all our minds' perception.

Everything we experience is filtered through our mental conditioning. In a sauna, for example, the same intense heat that we find oppressive outdoors on a very hot summer's day is now something we have paid money for. Maybe we go to work every day, to the same office, with the same people; on some days it's heaven and on other days it's hell. In a relationship, the same person can feel different to us every day – sometimes we love them, sometimes we hate them.

It is all down to mental attitude; there is nothing *out there* which makes us happy or unhappy. If that were true, then it would mean that happiness and suffering actually reside within the fabric of the physical objects around us; and then everybody who comes into contact with those objects would have identical reactions.

Thinking in this way can strongly motivate us to train our minds, as we see that the mind is the source of happiness.

The final question is: *What about meditation? How does* that *address the situation?*

If everything depends on our minds, then training the

mind should be a top priority in our lives. Meditation will give us the very thing we wanted in the first place: happiness.

If we take time to explore these questions regularly, seeing what answers come up in our minds and what our attitudes are, the questions themselves can skilfully back us into a corner where we realise there's nowhere else to go but back to the meditation cushion. We'll start to see that meditation isn't an option – it's a necessity.

JOYFUL ENTHUSIASM

Sustainable diligence comes from a place of intelligence and joy rather than from feelings of duty. If our practice is driven by 'shoulds', it becomes much harder to keep going.

I think that particularly in the West, people can have quite a grim attitude around anything religious or spiritual, where they might feel reminded of a sense of duty and guilt. Even though practising meditation is not a religious exercise, it can connect with the same parts in us that religion influences, and thus give rise to similar attitudes.

I've noticed people walking into temples and churches as if they're entering a courtroom to be examined for some kind of criminal wrongdoing. We wouldn't dream of walking into a church and throwing our heads back in laughter. But why not? Instead we tend to hang our heads and speak in hushed, ashamed tones.

When some people approach anything remotely spiritual they start to feel bad about themselves, as if there is something terribly wrong that needs to be cleansed or fixed. Interestingly, the Tibetan language has no word for 'guilt'; as a Buddhist culture, Tibetans have grown up with a sense of original goodness rather than sin. When Tibetan lamas began to visit the West in the 1960s to teach Buddhism, they were quite alarmed by the intense levels of self-loathing and guilt that they encountered in us. The Buddhist model of the mind is that it is ultimately and naturally pure, with our negativity and confusion simply like dust on a mirror. This creates a very different attitude towards spiritual practice, where the practitioner isn't coming from a place of thinking that there's something wrong with them that needs fixing.

I think it's because of this difference in view that I've noticed a more happy, lively atmosphere in spiritual environments in the East. Meditation is a training for the mind that is central to many traditions of the East; in itself it is not religious, but due to our habit of association, I feel that we in the West often bring to it a rather joyless attitude.

Sustainable diligence that energises the mind can only really come from a place of joyful enthusiasm. If we are practising like somebody miserably dragging a bag of rocks up a hill, then our diligence will keep falling apart. We could instead remember that meditation connects us with our essence, which is pure happiness, and that turning within will actually bring us what we wanted in the first place – the happiness that we've been seeking from the world around us.

The word diligence comes from the Latin *diligere*, which means 'to take delight in'. If we can view our practice as an opportunity rather than a duty, then diligence will arise as joyful energy rather than as a heavy burden.

ATTITUDE

Our attitude towards our meditation sessions can play a major role in giving us the energy to keep going. We struggle to meditate when the journey seems too huge and we don't know where to start.

If you want to cross a mountain at night,
you don't need to light up the entire mountain.
A torch will show you one metre ahead on the path:
it illuminates the next few steps.
Just hold the torch so it shines on to the path in
*   front of you.*

– Buddhist proverb

Reading this book might feel like you're facing a mountain – a lot of different ideas have been presented, and it may all feel too much – I don't want to give you indigestion! You can go back later and look into individual chapters, reflecting on them and only absorbing parts at a time, rather than feeling you need to take it all on board from day one in order to be able to meditate properly.

This approach can also mean practising short meditation sessions – then you'll be more likely to remain consistent and be able to practise every day. If you think, 'Oh no, I've got to do an hour of meditation', that thought in itself can make you want to run screaming for the hills. But starting with 5 or 10 minutes every day is very manageable. Then you can work up from there.

Sometimes you might want to attempt a longer session, maybe even an hour, but that hour, or whatever period of time you choose, can be broken up into smaller segments, where for two or three minutes you're focusing with strong precision, for example using the breath, and then you take a rest for the same length of time. During the rest period, you're not getting up and moving about, but you can just let the mind do whatever it wants during the 'break'. Then you can go back into a two- or three-minute period of deliberate focus, concentrating strongly but without tension. Alternating like that throughout the session can be very helpful; otherwise the session can feel like forcing a hyperactive child to sit still. We need to ease the mind into the practice so that it doesn't rebel.

Another thing you can try if you're struggling to stay motivated in your practice, is to place more emphasis on building the habit of dropping into 'micro moments' of awareness many times per day – practising mindfulness in daily life (for more on this see p. 88). In terms of overcoming resistance, this is like slipping the practice under the radar before you've had time to notice that you've done it. It's no longer a 'big deal', but is something quite natural. You can soon start to feel nourished and will want to do more. The mindful moments bring down cortisol levels, and you begin to feel better. Nobody wants to walk around feeling stressed all day, and so mindfulness becomes a huge source of relief. This could then inspire you to do more formal meditation sessions. After all, there are many ways to enter the house; if you can't manage the front door, just climb through a window. This approach is a little like that.

One of the main reasons people struggle to keep practising is when their meditation is about trying to silence the mind, which, as explained earlier, is a mistaken approach and becomes an incredibly harsh process. It's like forcing the mind into a box, similar to being unable to breathe; of course we would then resist wanting to meditate. It's important to think of meditation not as a restriction, but as a method for giving the mind total freedom – and that's something we certainly *would* want to do.

When we are grasping after results, that can also lead us to feel demotivated. We don't get an instant 'hit' from meditation like, for example, when drinking a strong cup of coffee, and so our addiction to a 'high' can make us less motivated to meditate. This is exacerbated by the emphasis on sensory stimulation which permeates our modern culture, as described earlier. It's important to see the meditation path as a way of life rather than expecting to 'feel' something from it, and it's crucial to avoid becoming impatient for results. People who exercise and keep jumping on the scales to weigh themselves, or constantly run to the mirror hoping to see changes, just end up feeling disheartened; it's more useful to keep going, with a patient attitude.

It's also highly beneficial to meditate when we feel unwell, exhausted or unhappy, as I said earlier. At those times, people often think 'I'll meditate when I feel better, otherwise it won't be a good session.' But that kind of thinking is a trap, as we are telling ourselves that our practice has to feel a certain way, which is a huge obstacle to maintaining diligence. Maybe we could instead start to view meditation in the same manner we would treat a friend. If we have a really good friend, it doesn't feel right to say, 'Sorry, but I'm not in the mood to see you right now.' Unconditional friendship means we are there for them no matter what. Meditation is all about non-judgemental presence and awareness. If we're sick, we're sick. If we're tired, we're tired. We simply need to be aware.

FEELING SLEEPY

When I give meditation classes, pretty soon many people in the room start snoring. I am not offended at all, as I know that people who are new to meditation, or who've meditated before but aren't maintaining a daily practice, will usually find that the first few sessions make them feel sleepy. Sitting down to meditate, they are quickly overtaken by powerful feelings of drowsiness. This can lead people to doubt whether meditation could really help them with their working lives, as it feels more like a way of knocking oneself out. This changes if we meditate regularly. The sleepiness happens because our bodies are used to being busy – even when sitting still, we tend to be doing something. To sit and do *nothing* is a new experience, something the body generally associates with sleep, and so we start to nod off. It is just like leaving a computer alone – it goes into 'sleep mode'. When we establish a daily routine of meditation, things change, as the body learns to associate that stillness with a training in awareness. I find that meditation sharpens my focus and makes me feel refreshed – it is not like drifting off to sleep or going into a trance. So the answer is simply to persist with the practice, and the habit of sleepiness will change.

That said, many people find that meditating last thing at night can help with insomnia. A lot of people tell me they find it hard to sleep – they can't calm down as their minds are racing with thoughts, or they wake up with a jolt in the middle of the night and have difficulty getting back to sleep. I often recommend that as they lie in bed, they practise the 'mindful body' exercise from Chapter Five (see p. 78). This may not send them to sleep straight away, but many people find that making a habit of the practice can really help to alleviate the insomnia. In many ways it is similar to the idea of 'counting sheep', which is simply about getting out of the cycle of one's own thoughts and instead focusing on something simple and calming. Practising mindfulness of the body means that we are focusing on physical sensations, feeling the body's weight against the bed and scanning through the different parts. This takes us away from our thoughts and into the calmness of the present moment.

If you feel sleepy during a daytime meditation session, it can be helpful to sit up even straighter, pulling your body up a little, and to look upwards in the direction of the ceiling, without tilting the head back. This can refresh your energy and wake you up. It's also good to make sure you're not sitting in a hot, stuffy room, but that there's some fresh air. Meditating after a heavy meal is not a good idea, as that's when we often feel drowsy anyway. In the four-year retreat we got up very early in the morning and had many lengthy sessions all day, some of which were three hours long. I remember feeling incredibly sleepy and desperately fighting to stay awake, but then I learned how to relax very deeply and not to *fight* the tiredness. That feeling of *trying* to stay awake is actually a form of tension. If you can relax deeply *into* the tiredness while maintaining awareness, it feels as if you've gone through a dark tunnel of exhaustion and have come out the other end feeling quite refreshed. Our awareness is never tired.

TOO MUCH ENERGY

Sometimes when meditating we can find ourselves at the opposite extreme, feeling quite agitated. The mind becomes very busy, as if it is racing about, and we feel very unsettled. We want to jump up and go off to do other things, and it feels as if we are battling our thoughts. The important point here is to remember that there is nothing wrong with thoughts; meditation is not about clearing the mind. There is no point in trying to push the thoughts away; instead we simply need to keep returning to the meditation focus when we realise that we got lost. It is important to remain patient and not to worry about the racing mind. If a session contains lots of thoughts, that doesn't define it as a 'bad' session.

If this situation persists, it can be helpful to meditate *after* a meal consisting of warm, nourishing food, and even to sit in a room which is a little warmer than usual. You can also relax your posture a little – not slouching, but just softening how you're sitting. Look down, but without tilting your head forward.

The main point, however, is to be patient and not to feel that a busy mind is your enemy. What truly counts is the awareness, whatever the mind is doing. Neither drowsiness nor agitation can affect that awareness, which is like the sky behind the clouds.

COMPASSION

As we saw in Chapter Nine, another factor that will boost our practice is compassion. If we're meditating with a sense that we are doing it for the benefit of others, we'll tend to feel more inspired and will want to put more effort into it.

If it's just for ourselves, we might think, 'Why bother?' This is often where people fall down with diets and exercise programmes, as they start to think, 'It's okay. I'll eat really bad food and just live with the consequences; I don't really care.' However, if we're doing something for others, we might feel more motivated.

If you're preparing a meal for yourself, perhaps you just throw any old thing into the microwave; but if you have people coming over for dinner, you'll want to make something really nice. Doing things for others can inspire us to be diligent.

In terms of meditation practice, if you can think that you are dedicating your practice to the development of compassion and the ability to help not only yourself but others too, it gives the entire process a far deeper meaning. You could start to feel a sense of value in relation to what you're doing, and a wish to do it well, as a gift to others.

MEDITATION EXERCISES

1. The four ways of changing the mind
Usually when we talk about changing our minds, we are referring to changing a decision, but here we are talking about a deep and sustainable shift in attitude. Regular use of the following exercise will help to energise your practice, keeping you motivated.

The method in this exercise is contemplation or 'analytical meditation', which means to think deeply about a topic, to develop insight.

There are four steps, but you don't need to do them all in one session; in fact, it's more helpful to spend entire sessions on each one. It's good to practise them over time, in the order presented here, as they'll build up your understanding in a helpful way.

Sit with the usual good posture (see p. 70). With analytical practices it's fine to close your eyes if you wish.

Generate the compassionate intention that you're going to meditate for your benefit and also for the benefit of others. You're dedicating your meditation training to the happiness of all.

Next spend a few moments being aware of your body – feel its contact with the chair, and then be aware of your feet resting on the floor. After that, begin the contemplation exercise:

i) **Confidence.** Reflect on human life's great potential. Think about how a person has a strong capacity to learn, do and achieve things. The fact that you have the inclination and time to meditate, means that you are a fortunate person who possesses a great treasure. Your life is filled with opportunities for finding true, lasting happiness, by learning how to work with the mind. Now that you have these keys, you simply need to use them. Building confidence in this way – feeling lucky and happy about your opportunity for mental transformation – can help foster a sense of joyful inspiration to meditate more regularly.

When you are ready to end the session – usually timed at 10 or 15 minutes, bring your focus to your body for a few moments, feeling its weight on the chair.

End with the usual moment of compassionate intention – cultivating the wish to dedicate your practice to all.

Below are the other steps in this series, and as already mentioned, it is good to spend entire sessions on each one, and to structure the session as explained above.

ii) **Everything changes.** This step helps you to
become more aware of impermanence. Reflect upon the
fact that absolutely everything changes – there is

nothing which remains the same forever. Living a life where your happiness depends on impermanent things means that the happiness itself never lasts. If you learn to turn within, you can find enduring happiness. This is why meditation is so important.

Think about how time is short and so it's better not to waste it. Let's engage with the path of meditation right now, rather than putting it off till later.

iii) **Actions lead to results.** Contemplate how the things that you do, say and think create habits. These habits cause you to continue to behave in similar ways, generating effects in your life and for those around you. If you train in mindful awareness, you can have the strength to transform negative habits, actively build more positive ones and become more mindful of your actions. This leads to a deeper appreciation of ethical living. Remember that practising regular meditation, and bringing mindfulness to your daily activities, helps you to create a happier life as negative habits diminish and you learn how to sow the seeds for happiness.

iv) **Happiness and suffering come from the mind.** For this exercise, ask yourself the questions which were described earlier in this chapter (see p. 220). Explore the answers that come up, and each time go a little deeper by questioning those answers.

Why do I do all the things I do? What do I really want to achieve?

What am I doing about that?

Is it working?

What are the true causes of happiness and suffering?

What about meditation? How does that address the situation?

2. Sky meditation

This exercise is best practised outdoors or by a window with a view of the sky.

Sit comfortably so that your body is in a balanced posture, and where you can see the sky. You could even lie on your back in the garden or a park.

Begin the session by remembering why you are meditating – to bring true happiness and freedom into your own life and the lives of others. In this way, you're setting a compassionate intention.

Look into the sky and notice its qualities. Maybe it's a clear blue sky, or perhaps there are clouds. Is it a night sky; are there any stars?

Try to get a sense that your mind is just like the sky – vast, open and limitless. As you look into the sky, feel that your mind mixes with it, you are 'becoming one' with it. All your thoughts, emotions and distractions are simply part of it, just like the clouds or stars.

The meditation focus is to look into the sky itself. Remember to blink whenever you need to and not to look directly at the sun! Whenever your mind gets caught up in thinking and you lose track of the meditation, simply return your attention to where your eyes are looking – the sky. You are looking beyond all those distractions, into the boundless sky.

There is no need to feel bothered by anything; you can simply let thoughts, emotions and distractions pass by like clouds; you don't need to get involved with them, as your mind – like the sky – is greater. The distractions themselves are insubstantial, just like clouds.

At the end of the session focus on your body for a few moments, becoming aware of its contact with the surroundings, and then remind yourself again of the compassionate intention which you established at the start of the session – the wish to bring ultimate happiness to others as well as to yourself.

Afterword

• • •

I wrote this book because I am fascinated by the question of happiness. I think we tend to look for it in places where we just won't find it, when it actually lies within us. The key to unlocking this is meditation.

I used to hate meditating. When I first became a monk, I saw meditation as a chore or a duty, and I was frightened of what it might show me. That all changed when I found out what to do with my unhappiness.

I have been astonished to discover that happiness is a choice. It is like flicking a switch within the mind. There is no magic or mystery to this, it is simply to be found in those small moments of awareness.

I hope that this book has inspired you to meditate. I truly believe that we are here to love and help each other, and the aim of this book is to offer some kindness in these difficult times.

Happiness is inside, waiting for you.

Acknowledgements

Several people made it possible for me to write this book.

First and foremost, I would like to thank my teachers, Akong Tulku Rinpoche and Lama Yeshe Rinpoche, who have given me everything and literally saved my life.

I want to thank my wonderful publisher Liz Gough, who hunted me down and believed in me from the start, and Imogen Fortes my brilliant editor. I'm also grateful to Sara Sjölund for editorial guidance and help with structure.

I would also like to offer sincere love and thanks to Allegra Wint, Catherine Brown and Ash Ranpura, all of whom provided top-quality advice; also to Ruby Wax, Chloe Roberts and Shareena Harnett, who have each helped me beyond measure.

Photograph © Steve Ullathorne

Gelong Thubten is a Buddhist monk, meditation teacher and author from the UK.

He was educated at Oxford University, and became an actor in London and New York. At the age of 21 he suffered from severe burnout and a life-threatening heart problem. This dramatic wake-up call led him to join Kagyu Samye Ling Tibetan Buddhist Monastery in Scotland, where he ordained as a monk.

The term Gelong means 'senior monk'. Thubten's training over the past 25 years has included spending over six years in intensive meditation retreats, the longest of which lasted four years, and he has studied under some of the greatest Tibetan meditation masters.

Thubten is a world pioneer in mindfulness meditation teaching, with over 20 years' experience working in schools, universities, hospitals, businesses, prisons and addiction counselling centres. He works with major corporations such as Google, and is regarded today as one of the UK's most influential meditation teachers.

He teaches mindfulness to medical students and has lectured at Oxford University and for the United Nations. He and the neuroscientist Ash Ranpura collaborated with Ruby Wax on her bestselling book *How to be Human: The Manual.*

Funds raised from Thubten's work are donated to charity, to establish meditation centres which benefit local communities. Thubten has set up a number of outreach projects, bringing mindfulness to some of the most deprived areas in the UK.

www.gelongthubten.com
Instagram: gelongthubten
Twitter: @Gelong_Thubten
Facebook: GelongThubtenOfficial